The
BASIC MEETING MANUAL

The
BASIC
MEETING
MANUAL

For Officers and Members of Any Organization

Thomas Nelson Publishers
Nashville • Camden • New York

Published in Nashville, Tennessee, by Thomas Nelson, Inc. and distributed in Canada by Lawson Falle, Ltd., Cambridge, Ontario.

Printed in the United States of America.

Library of Congress Cataloging-in-Publication Data
Main entry under title:

The Basic meeting manual.

Includes bibliographies
    1. Meetings—Handbooks, manuals, etc. 2. Public
speaking—Handbooks, manual, etc. I. Thomas
Nelson Publishers
AS6.B35   1986   658.4'563   86-2409
ISBN 0-8407-4154-5

CONTENTS

Contributors and Editors vii
Illustrations viii
Introduction ix

PART ONE: Basic Organizational Structure and Parliamentary Procedure 1
1. Starting a New Group 3
2. Ground Rules for an Organization 9
3. Internal Structure 17
4. Business Matters 48
5. Parliamentary Procedure: Background and Guidelines . 59
6. Structure of a Meeting 67
7. Five Classes of Motions 82
8. Special Events for an Organization 117

PART TWO: Basic Public Speaking 135
9. Meeting Your Speaking Needs 137
10. Gaining Confidence 141
11. Analyzing Your Speaking Situation 145
12. Selecting Your Topic 151
13. Preparing to Do Research 155
14. Gathering Your Material 167
15. Writing Your Speech 177
16. Practicing Your Speech 192
17. Presenting Your Speech 198

PART THREE: Guidelines and Samples for Specific Speaking Situations 207
18. Leading the Pledge of Allegiance to the Flag 209
19. Introducing a Speaker 211
20. Presenting a Gift or Award 215
21. Accepting a Gift or Award 218
22. Delivering a Eulogy 220
23. Commencement Address 222
24. Inspirational Speech 225

25. Speech of Welcome 227
26. Response to Speech of Welcome 231
27. Speeches for Patriotic Occasions 232
28. Speech of Tribute 242
29. Speech of Dedication 244
30. After-Dinner Speech 246
31. Speech for High School or College Reunions 249
32. Toasts—Wedding, Retirement, and Testimonial 251
33. Making Announcements 255
34. Praying in Public 256

PART FOUR: Topical Quotations for Speakers 261
    Notes 321

CONTRIBUTORS AND EDITORS

Mary Bray Wheeler
Managing Editor

Barbara Friend   Genon Hickerson Neblett
Margaret P. Hogshead   Marlene Patterson
Teri K. Mitchell   Julie M. Smithson
J. Clayton Stephens, Jr.

ILLUSTRATIONS

Sample Forms

1. Job Analysis 34
2. Agenda Planner 35
3. Minutes Form 36-37
3A. Sample Minutes 38-39
4. Treasurer's Monthly Financial Statement 40
5. Ledger Sheet 41
6. Authorization for Payment 42
7. Year-end Statement of a Church Treasurer 43-45
8. Year-end Treasurer's Report 46
9. Report of Committee 47
10. Budget for a Parent Organization in a Small School ... 56
11. Proposed Annual Budget of a Small Church 57
12. Proxy Ballot 81

Simplified Chart of Motions

1. Privileged Motions 111
2. Subsidiary Motions 112-113
3. Incidental Motions 114-115
4. Unclassified or Miscellaneous Motions 116

INTRODUCTION

PERHAPS YOU have just been elected president, secretary, or treasurer of the P.T.A. group at your child's school. You're unclear about the exact nature of your duties. Or, maybe you have been asked to bring a devotional at the next meeting of the civic club to which you belong. You wonder how to go about preparing a brief inspirational talk for such a meeting. This book is designed as a practical answer to needs such as these.

The Basic Meeting Manual is filled with helpful hints, suggestions, and guidelines on how to establish a new group or voluntary organization, write a constitution and bylaws, and conduct regular meetings. Duties of the officers of such a group are explained in clear, understandable language. Samples of many typical documents used, such as annual budgets and minutes of meetings, are included to show exactly how these reports should be compiled.

Since public speaking is an essential skill in voluntary organizations, a large part of the book is devoted to this function. You should find this material helpful in preparing speeches for specific purposes. The last section of the book contains hundreds of quotations on scores of popular topics. These interesting and inspirational items should help you in your speech preparation.

Voluntary organizations are a significant force in modern society. *The Basic Meeting Manual* was compiled with one clear purpose in mind—to make you a more effective leader and member of the voluntary organizations in your life.

PART ONE:

BASIC ORGANIZATIONAL STRUCTURE AND PARLIAMENTARY PROCEDURE

CHAPTER 1

STARTING A NEW GROUP

HUMAN BEINGS, it has been said, are social animals, and indeed one of the first signals of advancing civilization is the banding together of groups of people to achieve a common goal.

Today people form innumerable groups for social, educational, religious, civic, political, philanthropic, and self-improvement purposes. But what all successful organizations have in common is a clearly defined reason for being and certain concrete ways to operate, that efficiently, economically, and equitably help achieve their goals.

PLANNING

Whatever the impetus for starting an organization, a certain amount of sensible planning is required. Although one person can sense a need and be the initial motivator, it usually takes several people to put a plan into action. Before the organizational meeting the persons responsible for the club have several obligations. They must choose a date and place for the meeting, picking a day and time when most of the prospective members can attend, at a location that is convenient and has parking available. While a meeting can be in a home, it can also be held in a bank's community room, a school, a library, a church or other public facility. Definite arrangement should be made with clearly understood requirements, such as adequate seating, a podium, and a public address system, if necessary.

Notification of prospective members should be planned, allowing ample latitude for people to schedule their time. Methods of notification will vary depending on the type of club. They can range from a series of telephone calls to taking out large advertisements in local newspapers.

Most important is to give serious thought to the nature, objectives, and possible activities of the group so that they can be communicated effectively to the proposed members. Some preliminary investigation could be made into requirements for becoming a nonprofit, tax-exempt corporation, if that is applicable. The organizers should think through some general guidelines for discussion at the first meeting to aid the bylaws committee, which should be appointed then, to facilitate getting the group into immediate action. They must also decide who will call the initial meeting to order, who will nominate a temporary presiding officer, and who will explain the objectives of the society.

THE FIRST MEETING

When the appointed meeting hour arrives, it is wise to delay the start for ten or fifteen minutes to give the people an opportunity to become acquainted with each other. Then the person chosen to call the meeting to order should stand, get the attention of the group, and say, "The meeting will please come to order; I move that _____ act as temporary chair." The motion should be seconded and put to vote; then after its adoption the person elected is asked to come forward and take the chair.

An alternative is to call for nominations from the floor. Someone should rise and place a name in nomination. No second is required, but one or two people can say, "I endorse the nomination." The one who called the meeting to order then says, " _____ is nominated. Are there any further nominations?"

If there are several candidates, the election should be by ballot. However, if there is only one, the presiding officer can take a *via voce* (by voice) vote, saying, "All those in favor of electing _____ for chairman say aye." After the affirmative vote, the presider says, "Those opposed say 'no.' " If the majority is in the affirmative, the presider declares the nominee elected and asks that person to assume the chair.

The newly elected *temporary* chairperson then says, "The first business in order is the election of a temporary secretary." Upon election, the secretary should pass around a sheet of paper for those present to sign, giving names, addresses, and telephone numbers.

The chair should explain or call upon someone else to explain the reason for the group's formation. The objectives and proposed activities of the club should be clearly and simply explained, with opportunity for those present to introduce additional ideas. After a short discussion someone should offer a resolution proposing the formation of the club. A member will obtain the floor and say, "I move the adoption of the following resolution: 'Resolved, That....' "After reading it, the member hands it to the chair and another member says, "I second it." Then the chair says, "It is moved and seconded to adopt the following resolution: '....' The question is on the adoption of the resolution. Are you ready for the question?" This asks if those present are ready to put the question to a vote. The resolution is now open to debate and amendment. If there is no discussion, the chair takes the vote.

Once the group is on record as formally deciding to organize, a member should make a motion such as the following: "I move that the chair appoint a committee of (five) to draft a constitution and bylaws and report at an adjourned meeting."

(An *adjourned meeting* is simply another meeting that the club decides to hold before they adjourn.) When the motion is seconded, the chair should state it and conduct the vote. Upon passage the chair appoints the committee and then inquires if there is any further business to come before the group.

If the club is going to own property or wishes to be declared a nonprofit organization, certain legal requirements must be met and the club constitution and bylaws must be in compliance. Sometimes the wording of bylaws prevents tax-exempt status, whereas a simple change in phraseology meets the criteria. A committee to research this would facilitate writing the bylaws, although they can always be amended later.

One of the first items of business to confront a new organization is the matter of finances. Within the framework of the club's objectives, initiation fees and membership dues must be discussed and the amount set stipulated in the bylaws. With no precedent to follow, a budget must be prepared to include possible initial expenses such as corporation fees, fees to lawyers and tax consultants, procurement of meeting space, and estimated operating expenses. Questions should be settled as to types of available membership—individual, family, corporate, honorary, etc. A committee can be appointed at once to investigate budgetary items and provide cost estimates. One of the first actions of the permanent president should be to appoint a budget chair, preferably someone with financial expertise.

When all business has transpired, someone then makes a motion to adjourn to meet at a certain time and place: "I move that when we adjourn, we adjourn to meet at...." This motion must be seconded, stated by the chair, and voted on. Upon adoption, the first meeting of the group is adjourned to meet in continuation at a specified time and place.

THE SECOND MEETING

At the second meeting, the temporary chairman calls the meeting to order at the stated time by saying, "The meeting will now come to order. The secretary will read the minutes of the first meeting." When the temporary secretary finishes, the chair says, "Are there any corrections to the minutes?" If someone calls attention to an error, the chair says, "Unless objection is made, please make the necessary correction." If there is no correction, the chair says, "The minutes stand approved as read."

The chair then states that the next business in order is the report of the chair of the committee on the constitution and bylaws. The scenario for adoption is similar to this. The chair of the committee says, "The committee appointed to draft a constitution and bylaws has agreed upon the following and has instructed me to report the same and to move their adoption." He then reads them and moves their adoption. It is advisable to distribute copies so the members can follow along during the reading. After the motion is seconded, the chair says: "It is moved and seconded to adopt the constitution and bylaws reported by the committee. The question is on the adoption of the constitution." The first paragraph of the constitution is then read and the chair inquires if there are any amendments offered for it. If one is offered, the chair says, "If there are no further amendments to this paragraph, the next one will be read." Votes are not taken on separate paragraphs. This paragraph-by-paragraph procedure is called "consideration seriatim." After all paragraphs have been read and any amendments have been offered, the entire constitution is open for amendment. Any paragraph may be amended and new paragraphs added.

When it appears that all amendments have been made, the chair says, "Are you ready for the question?" If there is no objection, the chair says, "All those in favor of adopting the constitution as amended say aye." After this vote the chair says, "Those opposed say no." Only a majority vote is required to amend a constitution before its adoption by a new organization.

Adoption of the bylaws comes next in a manner similar to the adoption of the constitution. However, no motion is necessary now as the motion to consider both constitution and bylaws was passed earlier.

The next business in order is the election of permanent officers, which must be done as prescribed by the constitution. Possibly the chair can appoint a nominating committee to withdraw at once to prepare a slate of nominees. Business may be transacted while the nominating committee is in session, or a recess may be taken. However, it may be necessary to hold another meeting to complete the election, so provision should be made to meet at a definite time and place.

Once the officers have been elected and installed, the new organization can begin to set up its functional framework and get on with the business for which it was begun.

NOTE: The term *annual meeting* is used in two senses. An association may leave the management of its affairs to a board, having only one general meeting each year. Other organizations that meet regularly designate one of those meetings as the *annual meeting* when officers are elected, final reports of standing committees are given, and the audited financial statement is read, in addition to usual business.

CHAPTER 2

GROUND RULES FOR AN ORGANIZATION

A CONSTITUTION and bylaws define for a group its overall purpose, establish its organization and management, and provide needed continuity. The distinction between the two is that the constitution usually states the focus of the group, gives the broad governing principles, and declares the important rules, whereas the bylaws detail the regulations to manage internal affairs and standardize meetings.

If an organization is large, it may be advisable to have both a constitution and bylaws. For instance, the National Honor Society has a constitution that all local groups must adhere to. Each chapter then writes its own bylaws that tell how the chapter operates in the specific school within the framework of the prescribed constitution. Small clubs can combine the two and adopt only a set of bylaws.

An incorporated society may substitute its Articles of Incorporation for a constitution and have its bylaws harmonize with the Articles.

THE CONSTITUTION

The constitution, if used in conjunction with bylaws, usually contains six Articles divided into sections:

Article I.   Name of organization
Article II.   General purpose
Article III. Definition of membership (active, associate, honorary, etc.)
Article IV.   Officers of the club
Article V.   Procedure for nominations and elections
Article VI.   Provisions for amending the constitution

BYLAWS

Bylaws for the preceding constitution would contain:

Article I.   Qualifications of members
Article II.   Meetings (frequency, provisions for special sessions, establishing a quorum)
Article III. Duties of officers
Article IV.   Executive Board
Article V.   Committees
Article VI.   Dues
Article VII. Parliamentary authority
Article VIII. Procedures for amending bylaws

If bylaws only are used, they should incorporate the articles found in the constitution.

RULES OF ORDER

Each organization should specify under which parliamentary authority it operates. *Robert's Rules of Order* is probably the best known and is the authority for this book. Others often used are *Sturgis Standard Code of Parliamentary Procedure* by Alice F. Sturgis and *Essentials of Parliamentary Procedure* by J. Jeffrey Auer.

AMENDING THE CONSTITUTION AND BYLAWS

To amend the constitution or bylaws, most organizations require that adequate notice be given to protect the rights of absent members and to allow time for reflection. This step may be taken either by mailing a notice of proposed changes or by deferring action to the next meeting after introduction of the amendment. Approval of amendments should be by two-thirds of the votes cast.

The motion to amend the bylaws comes under Unfinished Business. The presiding officer says, "The next business in order is the consideration of the amendment to the bylaws proposed at our last meeting." The secretary or the chairman of the rules committee reads the change. Then the chair calls for a motion for adoption. After it is seconded, the president says something such as the following: "The question is on the amendment to the bylaws to add to Article V a new section to be known as Section 4 as follows...." If there are no amendments to the proposed amendment, the president waits for the discussion to stop and says, "A two-thirds affirmative vote is required. Those in favor of adopting the amendment will rise." (Count made.) Then, "Those opposed will rise." The chair then announces the result. Unless the motion specified otherwise, the approved change goes into effect immediately.

STANDING RULES

Standing rules detail practical matters that are adopted when needed, without notice, by a majority vote at any regular business meeting. They may be suspended by a majority vote or they may be amended or rescinded by a two-thirds vote. Some examples of standing rules might be: 1. Meetings should begin at 7:30 P.M. 2. Meetings shall be adjourned no later than 9:30 P.M. 3. Members shall not bring children under ten years of age to meetings.

COMBINED CONSTITUTION / BYLAWS

ARTICLE I—Name
The name of this organization shall be _____ .

ARTICLE II—Purpose
The purposes of the organization are _____ .

ARTICLE III—Membership
Section 1. Types of membership shall consist of (active, sustaining).
    A. Active membership requires _____ .
    B. Sustaining membership requires _____ .
Section 2. Qualifications for membership are _____ .
Section 3. Application for membership must _____ .
Section 4. Annual dues shall be _____ , payable before the meeting of each year _____ .
Section 5. A member who resigns in good standing may _____ (reinstatement policy).
Section 6. A member who is dropped from the roll for nonpayment of dues may _____ (reinstatement policy).

ARTICLE IV—Officers
Section 1. Officers of this organization shall be a president, a vice president, a secretary, a treasurer.
Section 2. In case the office of president becomes vacant, the vice president shall automatically become president. A general election shall then be held to fill the vice president's position. A similar election shall be held to fill a vacancy for secretary or treasurer.

ARTICLE V—Elections

Section 1.

A. Officers shall be elected and installed at the annual meeting to serve for a term of one year or until their successors are elected.

B. A plurality shall constitute an election.

Section 2.

A. At the regular meeting held in (month) a nominating committee of three (3) shall be appointed by the president to prepare a slate of officers.

B. The nominating committee shall obtain the consent of the nominees to place their names on the slate.

C. No officer shall be eligible for consecutive terms in the same office nor be eligible for that same office except after an interval of two (2) years.

Section 3.

A. The nominating committee shall make its report at the annual meeting held in (month).

B. Nominations may be made from the floor.

C. Election of officers shall be by secret ballot.

D. Voting privileges shall (describe who may vote and how much each vote counts, if applicable to the organization).

ARTICLE VI—Duties of Officers

Section 1. The president shall preside at all club and Executive Board meetings; appoint the standing committee heads immediately after installation; appoint special committees; sign, with the treasurer, all checks; serve as ex officio member of all committees except the nominating committee.

Section 2. The vice president shall assume the duties of the president in her absence; automatically become president in case of death or resignation of the president; and serve as program chairman.

Section 3. The secretary shall record all proceedings of the meetings and Executive Board; handle all correspondence.

Section 4. The treasurer shall collect all dues and care for the club's funds; keep an accurate record of receipts and payments; submit a report at each Executive Board meeting; submit a financial report at each regular business meeting and an annual, audited report at the annual meeting.

ARTICLE VII—Meetings
Section 1. Regular meetings shall be held on _____ .

Section 2. Special meetings may be called by the president, the Executive Board, or upon request of _____ members in good standing.

Section 3. _____ members shall constitute a quorum.

ARTICLE VIII—Executive Board
Section 1. The Executive Board shall consist of the officers and chairs of the standing committees.

Section 2.
  A. Meetings of the board shall be held _____ .
  B. _____ members shall constitute a quorum.
  C. A meeting of the outgoing and incoming Executive Boards shall take place soon after election for transfer of files.

Section 3.
  A. The Executive Board shall have supervision over the affairs of the organization between meetings.

B. It shall see that the objectives of the organization are accomplished.

C. Each outgoing board shall leave in the treasury a sum of money equal to the unpaid bills and obligations plus an emergency fund.

ARTICLE IX—Committees

Section 1. The following standing committees shall be appointed: _____ .

Section 2. The president may appoint additional standing committees as the need arises.

Section 3. The president may appoint special committees as necessary unless this rule is suspended by majority vote.

ARTICLE X—Discipline

(Provision may be made here for dismissal of members and officers.)

ARTICLE XI—Parliamentary Authority

Robert's Rules of Order shall govern the proceedings of the organization.

ARTICLE XII—Amendment

These bylaws may be amended by a two-thirds vote at any regular meeting provided the amendment was submitted in writing at the previous regular meeting.

ARTICLE XIII—Dissolution

If the organization is dissolved, all assets of the organization shall be divided equally among the members in good standing after all bills are paid.

Here are some suggestions to keep in mind while preparing

bylaws. They should be flexible to avoid frequent amendment or revision, although a periodic review of the bylaws will determine if they need revision. Language should be very simple and clear, and all essentials for conducting business should be covered. Provision should be made to deal with unpleasant situations before they occur, as in the matter of disciplining members, dropping them from the rolls, removing officers who do not perform their duties, requiring outgoing boards to leave a set amount in the treasury, and spelling out guidelines for transition of office.

CHAPTER 3

INTERNAL STRUCTURE

EACH OFFICER in an organization has specific duties and obligations, and each one should be aware of this relationship with the others. While the bylaws give some direction to the officers, a detailed job description for each office and important committee chairmanship should be developed so there will be no misunderstandings and the business of the club can proceed smoothly from one term to the next. It can be helpful to hold a retreat or workshop to study the bylaws and job descriptions, to set goals, and to make specific plans for the coming year.

JOB ANALYSIS

This description should include the title of an officer, definition of a job, qualifications necessary, person to whom officer is responsible, persons responsible to the officer in question, specific duties and how to perform them, often with a timetable and assignment of priorities (see illustration 1 on page 34).

While each new administration should meet and determine its own key objectives, a master schedule of necessary functions should be on file. For instance, the chairman of the Worship Committee of a church should know that in August an asking budget should be prepared, in September the committee on Advent plans should be appointed, in October plans should be finalized for Advent, and in November the Lenten committee should be appointed.

To develop a schedule check the constitution and bylaws, previous minutes, ask last year's officers, and examine the general calendar if part of a national organization. Regular meetings of standing committees appear on the schedule as well as monthly business meetings and the planned programs.

PRESIDENT

The term *president* is most often used for the highest ranking officer because *chairman* or *chairwoman* (both are historically sound titles dating from the seventeenth century) usually refers to the highest ranking committee member. The term *the chair,* used in the same sense that *the Crown* is used for a king or queen, is frequently used to mean the presiding officer. To stress the impartiality of the chair, the presider should always refer to herself by that term rather than use the pronouns *I* or *me.* The term *presiding officer* is not a title, nor does it refer to an officer, but is simply the term used for whoever is conducting the meeting. One does not say "Madam Presiding Officer," but rather "Madam President."

The president is the key to a well-run organization. She should be skilled at delegating responsibility without losing authority, should conduct meetings in an orderly fashion, and give each member fair opportunity to discuss and vote so the democratic process is achieved for a proper and purposeful outcome. Tact, humor, sincerity, patience, self-control, open-mindedness, humility, and fairness are good qualities to possess. The president should be dedicated to the ideals of the group and be willing to work hard.

It is essential that a president be thoroughly knowledgeable about the organization's history, purpose, and current activities. A new president should prepare for the office by reviewing the constitution and bylaws, and by studying all files and reports. The president should also take time to reflect on personal goals and aspirations for the forthcoming term and communicate them to the Executive Board and the membership, who in turn may have their own ideas to communicate. All committee or board appointments as provided in the bylaws should be made in a responsible manner. Thorough knowledge of parliamentary procedure is a must.

A specific duty of the president includes establishing an agenda before each meeting in time for it to be shared with the membership. (See illustration 2 on page 35.) Also the president is ultimately responsible for providing a comfortable, convenient physical setting for the meeting. To each meeting the president should bring a copy of the constitution and/or bylaws, a copy of the parliamentary authority, a quick reference card of motions in order of precedence, a list of all committees and committee assignments, and a memorandum of all business to be transacted.

The president calls the meeting to order on time, follows the proper order of business, states all questions before putting them to a vote, announces the results of each vote and the next order of business, and in a fair and impartial manner keeps the business moving to adhere to a time schedule. If questions should arise regarding parliamentary procedure, the president or parliamentarian (if there is one) should respond clearly and refer to the prescribed rules of order.

The gavel, traditional symbol of authority, is used with one tap to call the meeting to order, followed by the statement, "The meeting will please come to order." Occasionally a firm tap may be needed during a meeting to secure order. A final tap announces adjournment.

Normally the president stands while conducting business such as stating a motion, putting a question to vote, or announcing the result. During the reading of the minutes or a lengthy discussion, she may sit.

In a discussion sometimes the president has knowledge that other members do not have, so it is acceptable for the president to present facts, but he should always avoid stating opinions. The practice of leaving the chair to express a personal opinion on a controversial issue is not good leadership, as it is counter to the imperative of impartiality.

If the president must leave the chair for an emergency, he says, "Will the vice president (or some other officer) please come to the chair?" and hands over the gavel. When the president returns, the vice president says (at the first opportunity that does not cause disruption of business), "Will the president please resume the chair."

In voting there are certain prescriptions defined for the president. In case of a standing vote or a show-of-hands, the president may vote when there is a tie or when one more vote will make a tie. A motion receiving a tie vote is automatically lost unless the president cares to break the tie. When the president's vote will make a tie, he may vote to do so, thus causing the motion to be lost. The chair cannot vote to make a tie and then give the deciding vote. When the vote is by ballot, the president may vote during the balloting but not after the ballots are counted. If the result of a ballot vote is a tie, the vote is automatically lost.

Another responsibility of the president is to attend all meetings. If it is necessary to be absent, the president should inform the vice president, allowing as much notice as possible. If the vice president cannot attend, the secretary calls the meeting to order and a chairman *pro tem* is elected.

VICE PRESIDENT

The vice president should have the same qualifications as the president and assumes the office if it becomes vacant, un-

less otherwise stipulated in the bylaws. Many clubs traditionally use the vice presidency as a training post for the
presidency. When presiding, the vice president is addressed
as "Mister President" or "Madame President."

Although the vice president may serve in any number of
leadership and managerial ways, frequently the vice president
is program chairman, an important function for the vitality of
a club. The vice president may want to work with a committee and/or receive membership input as to desirable programs
to plan. Past programs should be reviewed to avoid duplica-
tion, and the schedule should be established well in advance.

The program chairman should make definite commitments
with outside speakers to include any compensation, including travel, housing, or meals, and inquire if any special
equipment such as movie or slide projectors should be provided. If arrangements are made far in advance, verification
and reminders should be made closer to time. It is always
prudent to have some backup plans in case of emergency.
The agenda for the meeting can be set so the program comes
first, to save the guest from having to sit through lengthy club
business.

The program chairman arranges for any advance publicity;
meets the speaker; makes introductions by using biographical
information previously supplied; thanks the speaker after-
wards, both at the conclusion of the program and later by
mail; and sees to all details such as presentation of the
honorarium and sending along clippings from the newspapers about the event.

SECRETARY

In large organizations where there is much correspondence, secretarial duties may be divided between a recording
secretary and a corresponding secretary, but smaller clubs
combine the two functions.

The recording secretary keeps the records of the organization, including taking notes of proceedings, writing them as formal minutes, preserving them, and reading them at the next meeting. (See illustration 3 and 3A on pages 36-39.) The role also entails maintaining an accurate alphabetical list of membership, a file of reports of boards and committees, a list of current business for agenda preparation, and a reference book containing the constitution bylaws, standing rules, photocopies of the charter, tax-exemption letters, and contracts. Vital information such as the location of the club's safety deposit box, the location and number of its key, and a list of the contents of the box should also be included. The treasurer maintains the comprehensive financial records, and each committee chairperson has charge of that committee's records.

The corresponding secretary answers all general correspondence. Officers attend to correspondence directly related to their work as do committee chairperson. Besides reading correspondence at the meetings as directed by the president and answering it, the corresponding secretary maintains files of all correspondence along with carbons of letters received for as long as practical and necessary. The corresponding secretary may also be in charge of sending appropriate cards and letters for illness, sympathy, birthdays, and thank you notes for special services. Unless other provisions are made by the club, the corresponding secretary types and distributes the agenda, both for Executive Board meetings and for regular meetings, notifies the board members and club members of meetings, and provides the necessary club publicity in the media. The secretary also notifies club members who were absent of their appointment to committees.

Minutes

Club minutes are the official record for the organization, a reminder for members in attendance, and a summary of action taken for absentees. Without good minutes some business might be repeated, essential matters be left undone, or hazy memories warp recall of actual accomplishments.

In the absence of the recording secretary the presiding officer, with approval of members present, appoints a temporary secretary (secretary *pro tem*) to take the minutes.

Coming from the Latin word meaning "small," minutes are just that, a concise record of what was done, not what was said. A common failing of secretaries is to take too many notes, and then to write them up with editorial comment. For instance, it is not good form to call a program "interesting" nor refreshments "delicious." It is important that the secretary take accurate notes (often with the help of a standard form, certainly with the agenda) at each general meeting, at Executive Board meetings, and at any other meetings designated by the president, that they be transcribed accurately and free from bias.

A copy should be sent to the president as soon as possible to help in agenda preparation for the next meeting. In the final official form, minutes are usually typed, then placed in the minutes book. The right margin should be wide enough to allow space for any needed corrections or additions. A short subject heading should be placed beside each paragraph in the left hand margin.

The first paragraph should contain the kind of meeting (regular or called), the name of the organization, date, time, place, and name of the presider. Each new subject requires a separate paragraph with reports of officers, boards, and committees noted along with names of persons who gave the reports and the action taken. There should be a new paragraph for each main motion and each motion bringing the main motion back for action. Exact wording should be recorded for each main and restoratory motion, along with the name of the person making the motion but not necessarily the name of the seconder. Disposition of each motion should be recorded, with the number of votes on each side if the vote is counted.

Also included in the minutes are points of order and appeals, with reasons for the chair's ruling on them. Record is made any time a club discusses business in a committee of the whole, but summaries of speakers' remarks are not given.

The name and subject of the program is given, but no summary is made of it. Last comes the hour of adjournment and under that the name of the secretary. Using the phrase "respectfully submitted" is now considered obsolete.

All motions should be written and given to the secretary for ease in exact transcription.

After the secretary has read the minutes of the preceding meeting, the president asks, "Are there any corrections to the minutes?" Any member who notices an error or omission speaks up. Then the president says, "There being no further corrections, the minutes are approved as corrected." In case there is major disagreement over the correction, a vote is taken with the majority choice declared the official correction. Minor changes are inserted in ink in the right margin and initialed by the secretary to show they are official. Major changes should be in an appendix with a note in the original referring to them.

After the minutes are approved, the secretary writes "approved" and the date to the left of his signature.

TREASURER

Since the treasurer is custodian of an organization's money, bonding is usually required if large sums are handled, but most small organizations do not require it. Specific duties vary from club to club, but common to all is the fact that the treasurer receives funds and disburses them. Therefore, essential items for the treasurer are an account book, checkbook, receipt book, and a file. Often checks must be countersigned by the president also. It is a good precaution to have signatures of the vice president and recording secretary on file at the bank for use in emergencies. The treasurer is usually authorized to pay routine bills that have been budgeted and approved, but large items and other requests must have special approval by the Executive Board. Receipts should be given and received whenever money changes hands.

Bookkeeping and auditing practices depend on the size and nature of the organization. Some require very complicated accounting procedures, but generally for small clubs a simple system is sufficient. Records of all receipts, deposits, and disbursements should be accurate and up-to-date, and the checkbook should be balanced monthly.

At each regular business meeting the treasurer should give the balance on hand at the beginning and end of the reporting period. A detailed report showing an itemized list of receipts and disbursements should be submitted, properly audited, at the annual meeting, which is usually the final meeting of the year. (See illustrations 4-8 on pages 40-46.)

One or more auditors may be elected or appointed by the club to look over the books before the final report at the annual meeting. This measure is for the protection of the treasurer as well as for the good of the club. Large organizations use professional accountants, but all auditors should affix at the bottom of the report a signed statement certifying that the books have been examined and found correct.

The treasurer's report at regular meetings is never approved. Only auditors can approve what the treasurer does. Instead, after the report is given to let the membership know the financial condition of the club, the president simply says, "You have heard the treasurer's report; it will be placed on file." At the annual meeting after the audited report is given, the president calls for a motion to adopt the report, which carries with it approval of the treasurer's report, if it was correct. If the treasurer's report is cited as in error, the treasurer is directed to correct it.

Other functions of the treasurer include keeping accurate records of dues that members pay, issuing reminders of dues that are delinquent, and advising members who are being dropped for nonpayment, if that is club procedure. A card file is a good way to keep membership lists up-to-date.

PARLIAMENTARIAN AND SERGEANT-AT-ARMS

Some organizations elect or appoint a parliamentarian, someone who is thoroughly conversant with parliamentary practice and with the club's bylaws, to sit near the presiding officer and advise on procedure when necessary.

Another office is sergeant-at-arms, either elected or appointed, who acts as doorkeeper, assists in keeping the room comfortable as to heat and air conditioning, helps count votes, and maintains order if necessary.

BOARDS

The term *board* can refer to different kinds of executive groups, although each board usually is constituted to attend to business matters that need not be brought before the entire membership. Some clubs formed for social, recreational, or mutual interest purposes have members who prefer not to be bothered by business details, so a board of directors is elected which then divides into specific committees. Unless the members must be polled, perhaps in a homeowners association to find out how many would want a master cable TV installation, the board functions independently and reports once a year. At this annual meeting some new board members are elected to fill the vacancies of the specified number rotating off the board, the annual report is given, and recommendations are made for the future. In stock corporations, the board transacts most of the company's business, often with stockholders voting their proxy votes by mail and never attending corporation meetings.

In smaller clubs the Executive Board, Executive Council, or Cabinet transacts necessary business between club meetings, handles routine matters so as not to clutter regular meetings with minute details, and serves as a guiding force to recommend policies or activities, which are then presented to the membership for action.

Duties and membership of the Executive Board should be spelled out in the bylaws. If there is no provision for an Executive Board, the officers can constitute themselves as one. Like all officers and committees, the board must always act in line with the constitution and bylaws as well as with the laws of the state.

Frequently the Executive Board is made up of elected officers and chairs of the standing committees. Often the immediate past president is an ex-officio member to provide continuity and benefit of experience. The bylaws or the standing rules should state when the meetings take place.

Very soon after installation the new Executive Board should meet to study club bylaws and its own function and job description, as well as that of the officers and committee chairs who constitute it. It should project its goals and activities for the coming term. The new budget and program plans should be assessed. Then board recommendations should be presented for ratification at the next general meeting.

The overall term *goal setting* has four distinct components: establishing, planning, executing, and evaluating. The first step in establishment is to review the stated purposes of the organization so that the new administration's long range goals mesh with the *raison d'etre* of the group. Good ways to accomplish this can be through brainstorming, through small groups, or through use of questionnaires. Questions to be addressed include: How is the club now achieving its purpose? Where is it falling short? What areas need working on? What general goals should this administration target?

Once broad goals are set, then short-term objectives to further each goal can be established. These should also be written and understood by all. Specific plans for activities to further each component should be made detailing exactly what is to be accomplished, who is responsible, and when it will be completed. Provision should be made for progress reports and for a final evaluation of each activity.

Without a final evaluation of the original stated goals as achieved through the various activities, the goal setting process is incomplete. Future goals build on previous ones. Reasons for success or failure are valuable to assess, and projected plans depend on what has been accomplished.

For a board to function effectively, a systematic method of assessing committee activities should be devised. Before each meeting the board should have in hand each committee report from its previous meeting. (See illustration 9 on page 47.) Final year-end committee reports and recommendations serve as the basis for a new board's initial planning session. In turn, the Executive Board should not only set club policy and spearhead action, but should also review and evaluate its progress toward the objectives. The board is also responsible for overseeing the finances and business matters of the club and should be sure to leave a working balance in the treasury at the end of its term.

Cordial relations between the board and club members are extremely important for a vital organization. Members should never get the impression that the board is "running things" to their exclusion. Board members should always be conscious that the board is a facilitating body, and they should continually and regularly report board actions to the group and receive endorsements of policy.

Occasionally problems arise if a member of the board is inactive or aloof from decision-making. The president should be alert to these situations and try to solve them satisfactorily, by appointing an assistant or by dividing responsibility, or even by tactfully suggesting resignation. Such a predicament should not occur, however, as each officer and chair should be responsible enough to tender resignation if, for whatever reason, duties of the office cannot be fulfilled.

COMMITTEES

In a democratic organization, committees are the foundation for effective action, as that is where small groups of people work together on a specific task. The bulk of actual club work is done here to increase efficiency, and it also enlarges the base of operation by providing opportunity for service from a large number of people. It is excellent training ground for future officers.

A Standing Committee is one that is appointed for an entire administration to carry out certain duties specified in advance. A Special Committee is appointed as need arises to attend to a certain matter and then automatically dissolves when its function is complete. A quorum for a committee meeting is usually a majority.

Examples of Standing Committees are Budget and Finance (which the treasurer can chair), Program (often chaired by the vice president), Membership, Hospitality, Newsletter, Directory, Telephone, Public Relations, Annual Fund-raising. Examples of Special Committees include studying the advisability of a motion, nominating the slate of officers, preparing for a nonrecurring special event, auditing the books.

Since committee chairmen are often members of the Executive Board, clubs should consider carefully what to designate as standing committees. For instance, if fund-raising happens every year and is vitally important to the club's finances, the person in charge should be on the Executive Board. In some groups, the historian, librarian, parliamentarian, and auditor are elected; others have them as appointive positions and they are considered committee chairs even if only one person performs the function.

The bylaws usually give the president authority to appoint Standing committees. Taking into consideration the nature of the duties and the aptitudes of the people being considered, the president should appoint them immediately after installation. Some groups like to have all members assigned to some committee. However, thought should be given before doing this, as committees should be small enough to operate effectively with each working member suited for the task at hand. It is not advisable for one person to chair more than one committee or even to serve on more than one.

Usually the president appoints Special committees. However, if the bylaws stipulate this, in the absence of the president no committee could be appointed to deal with an urgent matter. A good way to prevent this inconvenience is to have the bylaws state: "The president shall appoint all Special Committees unless the rule is suspended by majority vote." Then when the president is not there, a motion can be made to suspend the rule and after a majority affirmative vote, the temporary presiding officer can make the appointments. It is a good idea to have an uneven number of people on a committee to avoid possibility of a tie vote.

Since many matters that come before a group need more investigation and discussion than can be done during a general meeting, referral to a committee is the best course of action. Committees can consider resolutions and reports, consider a subject and report recommendations for action, or investigate some business before action is taken by the group.

Here are ways to commit: "I move to refer the resolution to a committee (or to the Buildings and Grounds Committee)." The motion may give specifics such as "I move that a committee of five be nominated from the floor with instructions to report at our next meeting," or it may give the committee "full power to act." The committee is usually named immediately after action to commit. If the chair prefers time to consider the appointment, the names can be announced before adjournment, or the members can be named by general consent after adjournment.

A motion to refer to committee is one of the lower ranking subsidiary motions in parliamentary procedure. It can be made only if a motion to postpone indefinitely or to consider a main motion and its amendments are pending.

If the chair of a special committee is not named, the first one appointed should act as convener and call a meeting as soon as possible. Another chair could be elected by the group if it desires, or if the chair does not wish to make the report to the assembly, another member may be designated to do so.

Principles for effective committee operation include having an informal atmosphere at meetings with the presider allowed to state her opinions and to vote; all members understanding the job to be done and participating, with divergent views freely expressed; knowing the extent of authority and responsibility for the committee; developing a plan of action with specific assignments given to individual committee members; and preparing and delivering a final report.

A committee report to the membership should not be lengthy or detailed, and its content should be agreed upon by the members of the committee. It may be oral, written, or both, but a written copy signed by the chair should be given to the secretary. A typical report would be: "The committee studying ways to introduce new members to the congregation recommends adoption of the following resolution: Resolved,

That a new member tea be held at the manse June 3, 3:00 to 5:00 P.M. I move adoption of this resolution." No second is necessary because more than one committee member has agreed to it. The presiding officer then states the resolution and handles it like any other main motion. Note that committee reports begin with identification of the committee, are stated in the third person, and that the recommendation comes at the end.

Sometimes there is disagreement among committee members and some may wish to present a minority report. The general membership of the club is not obliged to hear this, and it must grant permission for the minority to present its view.

The order of business provides opportunity for Standing Committee reports. Often these are simple progress reports for information only, so they require no action by the assembly. Therefore, it is not in order for a motion to be made to receive the report (as it is received when presented) nor should a motion be made to adopt it (as this would unnecessarily restrict the group for action on a subject simply under discussion). After the report is given, the president simply says, "Thank you," or if it is in writing, "the report will be placed on file."

Evaluation reports at the end of a job or a term are helpful to provide continuity and to aid future committees. The Executive Board should decide how or if these should be presented to the full membership.

The president is often declared to be an ex-officio member of Standing committees. However, this position does not require attendance at meetings and is not included in the quorum count.

MEMBERS

Although much is written about duties and responsibilities

of officers, the members also have their obligations. Without them, there would be no reason for having officers, for there would be no organization. Officers are really only members with specific duties, and all members are potential officers.

Some duties of members are listed in the bylaws, such as dues payments, perhaps even attendance and work requirements. Certainly all members need to come to meetings regularly and punctually and should keep themselves informed of the activities of the group and participate in the business at hand. Good members understand the objectives of the club, are familiar with the bylaws and the rudiments of parliamentary procedure, and understand the limitation of their authority and actions. When puzzling business takes place, they request clarification and are not afraid to speak up and express opinions, but they accept the majority decision gracefully. Good members are loyal, enthusiastic, and responsible. If they accept a job assignment, they carry through to completion. However, if it becomes impossible to perform a function, because of health, job, or family reasons, they notify the president immediately. Sometimes clubs provide a way for members to be placed on an inactive list temporarily or to become permanent sustaining members who do not participate actively but who support the group financially. The courteous member always writes a letter to the president tendering resignation if that becomes necessary or asking for a change in status. Older members always warmly welcome new members and give them an opportunity to become comfortable, with chances to serve the group.

In return, club membership can give one opportunity to make new friends, a feeling of belonging, satisfaction in accomplishing a goal, a widening of interest, and the gaining of experience in leadership.

Illustration 1
JOB ANALYSIS

(To be filled in by each new officer and committee chairman at first planning session.)

Title of job: _____

What do the bylaws say about it? _____

How does my job mesh with the stated purpose of the organization? _____

What planning does my job entail? _____

What regular work does my job require? _____

What special tasks are anticipated? _____

What regular meetings do I attend? _____

When and where do they meet? _____

What records should be kept? _____

To whom am I responsible? _____

Who is responsible to me? _____

With whom do I work regularly on the job? _____

How does my job correlate with other officers and committees? _____

How do I get funding for expenses? _____

What written reports are required? _____

To whom do I give them? _____

What are the deadlines? _____

What special goals do I have for the job this year? _____

Illustration 2
AGENDA PLANNER

Meeting date: _____   Regular ( )   Special ( )

Meeting place: _____

Officers excused: _____

Guests expected: _____

Minutes, previous meeting ( ): _____

  Special meetings: _____

Correspondence: _____

Officers' reports:

  Treasurer: _____

  Other _____

Executive Board report: _____

  Given by: _____

Standing Committees:

  _____ Committee, _____ reporting

  _____ Committee, _____ reporting

Special Committees:

  _____ Committee, _____ reporting

Special orders:

  _____ Time specified: _____

Unfinished Business and General Orders:

_____

_____

New business:

_____ by _____

Announcements:

_____

Program:

_____

Illustration 3

MINUTES FORM—For Secretary to Use Taking Notes at Meetings

(*Allow more spaces for usual amount of business. If there is more than space allows, assign a number and record by the same number on a blank sheet of paper.)

Meeting Date: _____   Time: _____
Place: _____
Kind of Meeting: Regular ( )   Special ( )   Other ( )
Presider: _____
Number Present: _____   Quorum? _____
Members Excused: _____
Guests: _____
Minutes of Previous Meeting:
Approved as Read ( )
Approved as Corrected ( )
Dispensed with ( )
Corrections: _____
Reports of Officers:
    Treasurer: None ( )   To File ( )   Attached ( )
    Balance on Hand: _____
*Other:
*Correspondence: None ( )
    Item: _____
*Report of Executive Board: None ( )
_____ given by _____
    To File ( )   Attached ( )   To Enter in Minutes ( )

MINUTES FORM (Continued)

*Reports of Standing Committees: None ( )
_____ given by _____
_____ given by _____
*Reports of Special Committees: None ( )
_____ given by _____
Action: _____
*Unfinished Business & General Orders: None ( )
Action: _____
*New Business: None ( )
  "That _____
  Carried: ( )   Lost: ( )
*Other (Appeals, Points of Order)

_____

*Announcements: None ( )
_____ by _____
*Program: None ( )
_____ by _____
Adjournment at _____ , Chair ( )
On Motion of _____ Seconded by _____

Signed _____
                Secretary pro/tem

Illustration 3A
SAMPLE MINUTES

Minutes of the Regular Meeting of the _____ Club
Nashville, Tennessee
December 15, 1984

Call to order: The meeting of the _____ Club was called to order at 7:30 P.M. by President Joan Smith.

Invocation: Jane Brown gave the invocation.

Roll: Thirty-six members were present.

Minutes: The minutes of the preceding meeting were read; after a correction was made, they were approved as corrected.

Treasurer's Report: Treasurer Anne Lewis reported a balance on hand as of December 8, 1985, of $1182.50.

Correspondence: A letter from Anna Garrison was read.

Committee Reports: Spaghetti supper chairwoman Josephine White reported that the supper will be held March 13, 1986, in the school cafeteria.

Unfinished Business: Elizabeth Ashley, chair of the committee to which a motion to help defray expenses to the JCL national convention was referred, recommended

SAMPLE MINUTES (Continued)

the following resolution: "Resolved that the—Club pay expenses of the JCL sponsor and one member not to exceed $500 to attend the JCL national convention in June 1985." The resolution carried.

New Business: Melody Mansfield moved that the newsletter which has been going out once each semester to all parents and alumni be sent out once each six weeks. The motion was seconded and passed.

Announcements: President Joan Smith announced that the Buildings and Grounds committee will meet Thursday at 4:00 P.M. at the school.

Program: Jane Ellison introduced Mary O'Casey, sponsor of the Drama Club, who introduced members of the club who gave a Readers' Theatre presentation on the meaning of Christmas.

Adjournment: The meeting adjourned at 8:55 p.m.

(Signed)— _____
Recording Secretary

Illustration 4
TREASURER'S MONTHLY FINANCIAL STATEMENT
_____ **CLUB**

Date: _____

Receipts
Dues—	$180.00 for 36 members
Gift—	15.00
Sale of dried bean soup—	82.00
Total Receipts	$277.00

Disbursements
Beans for soup—	$25.87
Packaging for soup—	6.43
Postage for newsletter—	18.00
Total Disbursements	$50.30

Balance in Checking Account———		$ 278.16
Balance in Savings Account———		736.50
Interest Earned———		3.68
	Total	$1018.34

Illustration 5
LEDGER SHEET

Account _____ **Amount Budgeted** _____

Date	Transaction	Amount Received	Expended	Running Balance

Illustration 6

AUTHORIZATION FOR PAYMENT

_____ **CLUB**

Account: _____ Date: _____
(Name of Committee)

Requested by: _____
(Signature)

_____
(Title)

Purpose of Expenditure: _____

If no invoice or receipt can be attached, please give reason:

_____

Authorized by: _____
President

Amount: _____
Payable to: _____
_____

Check No. _____
Date of Check: _____

Illustration 7

YEAR-END STATEMENT OF A CHURCH TREASURER*

RECEIPTS	December	Yr. to Date	Budget
Pledges	$13,993.40	$137,978.27	$138,676
Gifts	197.01	1,687.63	1,500
Church School	57.56	550.32	700
Rent (by day school)	1,100.00	9,400.00	9,400
Building Use	-0-	450.00	375
Interest	894.89	1,975.30	1,200
Total	$16,242.86	$152,041.52	$151,851

DISBURSEMENTS

Budget and Finance

	December	Yr. to Date	Budget
Postage, Prtg., & Off. Sup.	$ 368.92	$ 5,926.88	$ 5,200
Miscellaneous	(2.70)	140.30	211
Pastor's Expense	-0-	406.48	500

Stewardship			
Budgeted Benevolences			
Local	1,420.00	5,848.42	5,830
AS&P	1,160.00	14,000.00	14,000
Building and Grounds			
Utilities	1,785.09	19,598.17	24,765
Benton Hall Utilities	490.00	4,089.75	2,264
Insurance	-0-	2,264.00	9,937
Maintenance & Equipment	1,603.03	11,469.75	2,000
Worship	79.74	2,031.23	1,987
Christian Education	227.61	1,762.18	1,104
Fellowship	49.47	1,161.77	171
Membership	-0-	71.31	
Personnel			
Salaries	4,425.80	55,245.90	55,652
Emp. Health, Dental & Ret.	358.09	10,127.98	10,366
Expense Allowances	962.51	11,561.94	11,550
Social Security Taxes	218.32	2,818.50	2,914
Escrow-Future Housing	83.33	999.96	1,000

Annuity-Retired Minister	200.00	2,400.00	2,400
Stewardship Campaign	-0-	151.00	-0-
Total Budgeted Expenses	$13,429.21	$152,075.52	$151,851

FUNDS SUMMARY—YEAR TO DATE December 31, 84

	General Fund	Non Budgeted General	Non Budgeted Bene.	Reserve Accounts	TOTAL
Cash Bal., Beg. Period	$ 1,035.42	$15,174.05	$3,697.15	$11,503.54	$31,410.16
Receipts	152,041.52	23,838.98	9,002.69	44,495.45	229,378.64
Disbursements	152,075.52	31,951.61	8,867.45	25,829.01	218,723.59
Cash Bal., End. Period	1,001.42	7,061.42	3,832.39	30,169.98	42,065.21

*This statement shows the financial picture. The same form produced each month is helpful for any Executive Board and can be used to show committee chairmen how they stand according to their budgeted allotments.

Illustration 8
YEAR-END TREASURER'S REPORT

Band Boosters Club

For year ending March 31, 1985

Balance on Hand April 1, 1984		$ 43.86
Receipts		
Dues	$864.00	
Spaghetti Supper	576.00	
Total Receipts		1440.00
(Total)		$1483.86

Disbursements		
School General Fund (for band)	1100.00	
Custodial Service for Spaghetti Supper	50.00	
Supplies for Spaghetti Supper	186.78	
Postage	36.00	
Total Disbursements		$1372.78
Balance on Hand March 31, 1985		$ 111.08
(Total)		$1483.86

Teresa Duke, Treasurer

Audited and found correct.
Jay Holmes
Robert Cullom
Auditing Committee

Illustration 9

REPORT OF _____ COMMITTEE

(To be turned into the secretary two days before each Executive Board meeting which is on the second Monday of each month.)

Date: _____

Chairman: _____

Members: _____

_____

Immediate Goals of Committee: _____

_____

Committee Activities Since Last Report (for information only): _____

_____

_____

Results of Activities: _____

_____

Specific Future Plans: _____

_____

Club Action to be Recommended by Committee: _____

_____

Financial Statement (if applicable): _____

_____

Comments: _____

_____

CHAPTER 4

BUSINESS MATTERS

INCORPORATION AND TAX-EXEMPT STATUS

IF THE club qualifies, there are distinct advantages in becoming a corporation and/or being declared a nonprofit tax-exempt organization. A corporation is a body of persons granted a charter legally recognizing them as a separate entity having its own rights, privileges, and liabilities distinct from those of its members. Each state has codes setting forth the legal requirements for incorporation, both for profit-making and for nonprofit organizations.

Advantages of becoming a corporation include having the power to acquire and convey property; protection whereby members cannot be sued and lose their personal assets for the debts of the club; right to bring legal action and to sue and be sued as a body rather than as individuals. A nonprofit organization has tax-exemptions from the Internal Revenue Service from state taxes, and from city property and sales taxes. Contributions made to it are tax deductible, and it is eligible to receive funding through grants from foundations and governmental agencies. It also receives bulk-rate mailing privileges from the postal service.

Obversely, there are restrictions imposed on nonprofit tax-exempt groups. The laws spell out specific limitations on such things as engaging in political activity for or against candidates, having membership standards that discriminate by race or sex, and having profits and benefits paid to members other than for salaries and expenses.

Laws vary from state to state on incorporation requirements, procedures, and fees required. Often there are stipulations as to the name of the organization, with restrictions on the use of some words, such as *federal, United States, trust,* and *cooperative.* Also, the purpose of the organization must be stated in the Articles of Incorporation with extreme care taken in the wording. For instance, the word *philanthropic* may be inadmissible, while *charitable* would be acceptable. A special committee should investigate incorporation and tax-exemption. Its duty would include proposing necessary changes in the constitution and bylaws to conform with the prescribed Articles of Incorporation or governmental regulations regarding tax-exemption.

While the simplest way to incorporate is to engage an attorney specializing in corporation law, this approach will be the most expensive. Although some legal assistance will be required, groups can reduce expenses by doing preliminary legwork. The first step is to write to the Secretary of State of the state which will do the incorporating for guidelines. Another aid might be the local library, which will have the necessary information or will direct the patron to another library having it, or the yellow pages of the telephone book for the county Bar Association, which could recommend legal aid groups.

To achieve tax-exempt status, the organization must investigate whether it is affiliated with another one that is already covered by a group-exemption letter, as this would automatically apply to the smaller group. However, the subgroup must mesh exactly with the parent organization, and failure to comply in every respect with its stated purpose can result in loss of the original tax-exemption.

The Internal Revenue Service is a good source to determine tax-exempt eligibility; it has booklets which apply to the specific type of organization under consideration. It is wise to scrutinize the constitution and bylaws; for statements found there, while seemingly innocuous to the lay person, can prevent qualifying on a technicality. The purpose of the organization must be described in a very specific and restrictive manner. If political activity is part of the group's function, proper documents can be obtained from the IRS to determine what is and what is not permissible regarding lobbying and tell exactly how and when the authorization forms must be submitted.

Processing the application will be expedited if the required Articles of Incorporation include how the group's assets will be disbursed should the club become defunct. Information detailing what beneficiaries are eligible to receive the society's funds should be predetermined. Although the bylaws should state this, inclusion in the bylaws is not sufficient for the IRS; the beneficiaries must also be spelled out in the Articles of Incorporation.

Because of the complex nature of this procedure, it is advisable after the preliminary fact-finding and the gathering of pertinent documentation to consult with someone knowledgeable in the field of tax-exemptions, such as a tax consultant or an attorney.

Once all the documentation is supplied, and if tax-exempt status is granted, an exemption letter will be sent effective as of the date of the formation of the organization. If taxes have been paid, a claim for refund may be filed.

Even though the group receives federal tax-exempt status, there are other federal taxes which must be paid and forms that must be completed for those taxes that are covered by exemption. Also, exemption from federal income tax has no connection with state, county, and local taxes.

Again, the IRS will provide, upon request, the proper pamphlets about what federal taxes the group is responsible for and how to pay them. If there are paid employees, their federal withholding taxes and social security payments must be made, although as a federal tax-exempt organization the society is exempt from payment of the federal unemployment tax.

State income tax laws must also be investigated. If the state has an income tax, application must be made to the proper state authority for exemption from payment of sales taxes. Each city, county, and state has its own laws regarding property taxes.

An application at the local post office can be submitted for a nonprofit bulk-rate mailing permit. It is necessary to supply copies of the exemption issued by the IRS, the Articles of Incorporation, the constitution and bylaws, and samples of bulletins and/or programs that illustrate the nonprofit activities.

INSURANCE, PERMITS, CONTRACTS

At some point most organizations will need to consider matters of insurance, permits, and contracts. The bylaws should specify who is responsible for entering into contractual arrangements and who may sign for them. In any event all legal documents should be kept in a safe place with their location known to the proper officers, and they should be checked on regularly, especially if renewal is necessary.

Consultation with an insurance agent will determine what coverage the organization will need. Insurance needs may include property insurance, protection of employees, automobile insurance for volunteers who use their personal cars, and blanket policies to cover specific events such as a fund-raising activity.

Local permits may be required for fund-raising activities

and for sales of food and beverages. The organization is responsible for checking with local authorities.

Nonprofessionals running small organizations often invite trouble by being too naive or trusting in making contracts. Agreements should be written, never implied or oral, with any changes made after typing initialed by both parties. If the club is contracting for meeting space, exact requirements should be spelled out: fees, deposits and their refund arrangement, dates, starting and ending times, obligations of both parties. In arranging for a public meeting room at a bank, school, or other community center, an officer or committee member should confirm that the date is placed on the institution's calendar.

Here are considerations to remember while arranging for meeting space:

1. Number of parking spaces, lighting, entrance authorization, loading and unloading facilities, need for police permits;

2. Physical arrangement of room, operation of air conditioning and heating, tables, chairs, podium, public address systems;

3. Restroom facilities;

4. Equipment, operation of stage and lighting equipment for performances or kitchen equipment;

5. Maintenance, who is responsible for setting up and then cleaning up;

6. Cancellation provisions and deadlines;

7. Responsibility for accidental damage; and

8. Fee payment, when it is to be paid, if a deposit is credited against payment or will be refunded, if custodial service is included in the rental agreement.

MANAGEMENT

To avoid any misunderstanding, job descriptions for employees, both permanent and temporary, should be written and agreed to by both employer and employee. This agreement should spell out salary and benefits, pay days, statement of starting and ending times each day, days and hours to be worked each week, vacation and holiday allotment, and description of work to be done.

Some organizations are really as intricate to operate as many money-making businesses and may even surpass many companies in size of paid staff and permanent facilities. These have their own well-established operational procedures. Other organizations, such as a cooperative swim and tennis club or a condominium owners' association, frequently employ a paid manager who works under the direction of the board of directors and carries out specified duties that are prescribed by the organization. Then there are small groups run by volunteers, and it is equally as important for them to devise efficient management systems so they will keep from eternally reinventing the wheel. For instance, the session of a church may deliberate over and over to establish guidelines for the use of the sanctuary for weddings simply because no policy book has been kept on past sessional action, and it is difficult to sift through volumes of recorded minutes. A new PTA president may be inundated with cardboard cartons containing a mass of miscellaneous papers that have been handed down through the years.

One solution is to set up a clearly defined filing system with provision for each officer at the end of a term to sort and then transfer records to the successor with a predetermined place for storage. While each officer can house records at home for the term of office, some groups prefer to rent ministorage space for outdated records that must be kept for governmental reports or because of historical value. Annually each officer should discard all working papers, duplicates, and extraneous material. Permanent and current files should be kept separate.

Important documents, such as insurance policies, tax-exempt data, Articles of Incorporation, deeds, contracts, and inventories of property, should be preserved in a safety deposit box with the presence of two designated officers needed to open it.

The president should have a file containing photocopies of the Articles of Incorporation and tax-exemption letters; the constitution and bylaws; all year-end reports of officers and committee chairmen; a current membership list with committee assignments; the current budget and financial statements; and important correspondence along with carbons of answers.

The recording secretary should have a file containing the constitution and bylaws, rules of order, and standing rules; current motions and pending business; the budget for the year; photocopies of contracts and insurance policies with list of renewal dates of all contracts and permits; the minutes book; and copies of officers' and committee chairs' reports.

The treasurer's files should contain: ledgers and checkbooks; canceled checks and bank statements; audit reports; budgets; copies of governmental tax forms that have been filed; a list of active and inactive members with dues payment record; paid bills for equipment under warranty and any valuable papers that might be needed for insurance purposes.

BUDGET

Operating on a sound fiscal policy is necessary for all organizations no matter what the size. A realistic budget must be prepared and followed, so the chair of the budget committee is an important assignment.

Each year before the first budget committee meeting all officers and chairs should submit a statement of their estimated needs. (See illustrations 10 and 11 on pages 56-58.) The committee chair should have checked the treasurer's records to make a list of regularly recurring expenditures and should have projected necessary increases. Thus a tentative budget can be set up, to be compared with a realistic assessment of project income. It may be necessary to cut requests so a balanced budget can be achieved, with a reserve fund always built in for emergencies. Fiscally responsible officers do not leave a totally depleted or debt-ridden treasury for new officers to cope with. Once the budget is established, the chair brings it to the Executive Board and then to the general membership for approval in accordance with the requirements of the bylaws. The treasurer, the recording secretary, and president should have copies of the budget, and it should be available upon request for any member to see. It is the duty of the president and the Executive Board to see that the budget is followed.

Illustration 10
BUDGET FOR A PARENT
ORGANIZATION IN A SMALL SCHOOL

Budget Categories	Income	Anticipated Expenses
Building and Grounds	_____	$ 300.00
Alumni Relations (includes newsletter)	$ 662.00	600.00
Finance Committee (candy sale)	1000.00	50.00
Sports Program	_____	1000.00
Hospitality	_____	300.00
Membership Dues	2240.00	100.00
Minority Recruitment	_____	120.00
Gifts to School General Fund	_____	1432.00
Total	$3902.00	$3902.00

Cash on Hand in Checking Account: $ 300.65
Cash on Reserve to be Maintained: $ 300.65

Illustration 11

PROPOSED ANNUAL BUDGET OF A SMALL CHURCH

BUDGET & FINANCE COMMITTEE
BUDGET RECOMMENDED FOR ADOPTION FOR 1985
DECEMBER 13, 1984

	LAST 12 MONTHS ACTUAL EXPENDITURES	1985 ASKING BUDGET	RECOMMENDED FOR ADOPTION 1985
Budget and Finance	$ 7,874	$ 7,000	$ 7,000
Building and Grounds			
Utilities	24,130	28,335	26,000
Insurance	2,264	2,500	2,500
Maintenance and Equipment	10,486	3,500	3,500
Grounds Maintenance	3,000	4,000	4,000
Repair and Replacement Fund	2,500	5,000	3,000
	(42,380)	(43,335)	(39,000)

(continued on page 58)

Christian Education	2,660	4,970	3,470
Fellowship	1,018	775	775
Membership	130	310	310
Worship	1,943	4,000	3,000
Stewardship	16,601	14,455	14,455
Personnel	84,868	87,187	86,620
TOTAL	157,474	162,032	154,630

EXPECTED RECEIPTS:

$ 1,500—Gifts
600—Church School
1,000—Interest earned
5,500—Rent
146,030—Pledges
$154,630

CHAPTER 5

PARLIAMENTARY PROCEDURE: BACKGROUND AND GUIDELINES

PARLIAMENTARY PROCEDURE is a set of established rules for the orderly and systematic conducting of business and discussions to reach decisions in an efficient and democratic way. It enables people to work together effectively in groups and is based on the concept of total participation so it guarantees the right to discuss issues, voice opinions, request information, and vote convictions, with majority rule prevailing. It insures orderly meetings if proper procedures and practices are followed by the officers conducting the meetings.

Its history is long and respected, for its antecedents are rooted in the ancient Athenian *ecclesia* (assembly) and the Roman Senate. While its name derived from the French verb *parler* (to speak), it developed in the British Parliament, in which its broad principles had been established by the 1600s. Hatsell's *Precedents* for the House of Commons in 1776 collected traditional rules into one code. The early American colonists brought the concepts of parliamentary law to the New World and patterned their deliberative bodies in conformity to it. As vice president and presiding officer in the Senate, Thomas Jefferson drew up the manual of parliamentary practice still used in Congress. Its aim, he wrote, is to insure "accuracy in business, economy in time, order, uniformity, and impartiality."

In 1876 Major Henry M. Robert, a United States Army engineer, became interested in correct ways to conduct his church business meetings. Drawing on the parliamentary procedures used by lawmakers, he prepared a set of rules suitable for ordinary citizens, and his *Robert's Rules of Order* has now become a standard authority.

Everyone who belongs to any group needs a fundamental knowledge of parliamentary procedure because it places an equal burden on members and officers to insure the democratic process in assembly. The chair should always insist on use of accepted practice as a guarantee that all rights are respected.

GLOSSARY

There are certain basic terms that should be understood by all.

Adjourn—To close a meeting

Agenda—A list of items to be considered at a meeting

Amendment—A change proposed or made in a motion, constitution, or bylaws

The Chair—The presiding officer (one "Addresses the chair" when speaking to the presiding officer)

Close debate—Ending discussion on a motion

Debate—Discussion of a motion ("decorum in debate" refers to observance of proper procedure and normal courtesy)

Dilatory motion—A meaningless motion that must be ruled out of order

Division—A vote count by show of hands or by standing

Ex officio—By virtue of office

Gavel—Small wooden hammer used by the presiding officer to call the meeting to order and to restore order

House—The assembly, body

Lay a question on the table—To put a motion aside to be considered later

Majority—More than half

Minutes—Official record of the proceedings of an assembly

Motion—A proposal that certain action be taken by the assembly

New Business—Business brought before the group for the first time

Obtaining the floor—Receiving the right to speak

Order of Business—Series of steps covered in a meeting from Call to Order to Adjournment

Pending question—Any motion open for debate

Plurality—The largest number of votes received by a candidate in an election involving three or more candidates

Point of Order—An objection raised by a member because of improper procedure or annoying remarks, requiring immediate ruling by the presiding officer

Previous question—A motion to end debate on a pending motion and to vote immediately

Privileged question—A request made by a member asking the presiding officer to deal with an emergency or other matters of general welfare

Pro and con—Arguments for and against

Pro tem—For the time being, acting during the absence of another, such as a secretary *pro tem*

Proxy—A signed statement transferring one's right to vote or participate in a meeting to another person

Question—The business before the House

Quorum—The number of members that must be present to transact business legally

Ratify—Refers to a motion to approve an action already taken

Recess—A temporary interruption

Seconding a motion—Shows that another member also approves

Unanimous consent—Refers to a request by the presiding officer on matters where dissent is not expected, such as approval of the minutes, also called *General Consent*

Unfinished Business—A matter carried over from an earlier meeting

GUIDELINES FOR MEMBERS

• The organization should be called by its correct title: club, chapter, society, session, council, etc.

• The presiding officer is called "the chair" and uses this phrase rather than "I." During meetings whoever is presiding officer is "President," or "Chair." It is correct to address the person in the chair as "Mr. President," "Madam President." A vice president who is presiding is called "Mr. (or Madam) President," but a temporary presiding officer is addressed as "Madam (or Mr.) Chair."

• Say, "I move," rather than, "I make a motion."

• Speak of the "maker of the motion" rather than "the mover of the motion."

• Say, "The president put the question to vote," rather than "The president put the motion to vote."

• Verbs used to amend motions are "to insert," "to add," "to strike out," "to strike out and insert," or "to substitute."

• Say "I second the motion," rather than "sustain" it.

• When the presiding officer asks, "Are you ready for the question?" it means, "Are you ready to have the matter put to vote?" If someone wishes to discuss the issue first, she should obtain the floor and state her case.

- To obtain the floor, rise (or raise a hand in a small group and wait for the chair to nod in recognition or say, "The chair recognizes Mr. Smith." Do not interrupt business at hand (except under special circumstances), and do not speak until recognized.

- When two or more rise about the same time to claim the floor, the general rule, all other things being equal, is that the member who rose and addressed the chair first after the floor was yielded is recognized. Anyone who rises before the floor is yielded is not recognized ahead of those who wait to rise and address the chair after the floor is yielded.

- It is out of order to stand for recognition when the floor is assigned to someone else.

- Although a member may vote against her own motion if she has a change of mind during debate, the member may not speak against that motion.

- A member cannot offer a motion to reconsider unless he voted on the prevailing side.

- Even after a motion to adjourn has been passed, the meeting is not over until the president taps the gavel and says, "The meeting is adjourned." It is courteous to remain seated and quiet until then.

GUIDELINES FOR THE PRESIDENT

- Always have a watch at hand. Start meetings on time and end them at a reasonable hour.

- Use the gavel sparingly; one quiet tap is usually sufficient to begin the meeting, to restore order, or to signal adjournment.

- Have a desk at the front of the room with two chairs, one for the secretary and one for use by the president when it is in order to sit.

- Stand while stating a motion, putting a question to vote,

announcing the result, and speaking upon an appeal. It is permissible to sit during the reading of the minutes, for any lengthy report, or when the floor has been assigned to a member.

• While presiding, speak in the third person: "The chair appoints...."

• Preside fairly and impartially at all times. In debate call on speakers alternately for and against the issue, if this can be judged.

• Avoid hurting members' feelings by making statements such as "You are out of order." A person is never out of order; an action or a motion is. Try tactfully and courteously to suggest the proper course of action or motion to use.

• When a question is undebatable, do not ask, "Are you ready for the question?" State the motion and take the vote.

• When taking a rising vote say, "The affirmative has it and the motion is adopted," or "The negative has it and the motion is lost." Do not say, "The ayes have it." (In referring to votes the word is pronounced "I.")

• Always allow for a negative vote: "Those opposed say no." Phrases such as "contrary" or "show by same sign" are poor form.

STEPS NEEDED TO OBTAIN ACTION OF THE HOUSE

Ordinarily eight steps must be followed to obtain action of the House.

1. A member rises and addresses the chair.
2. The chair recognizes the member.
3. The member makes a motion.
4. Another member seconds it if it is the kind of motion requiring a second. It is not necessary to obtain the floor to second except in a very large group. The seconder merely says,

"I second it." The chair may ask, "Is there a second?" To say, "Do I hear a second?" is silly because who knows what the chair has heard. It makes a club meeting sound like an auction.

5. The chair then states the motion: "It has been moved by Mrs. Brown and seconded by Mr. Lewis that...."

6. If it is a debatable motion the president says, "Are you ready for the question?" (If the chair feels that the members do not understand this terminology, she should ask, "Is there any discussion?") When the debate seems to be over, the chair says again, "Are you ready for the question?" If the motion is not debatable, the chair puts the matter to a vote at once without asking if the members are ready for the question.

7. The chair puts the question to vote by saying, "The question is on the adoption of the motion to....As many as are in favor of the motion say aye." After the affirmative vote, the chair says, "Those opposed say no."

8. The chair announces the result: "The ayes have it; the motion to...is adopted."

THE EFFECTIVE MEETING

To be effective an organization must have well-planned meetings. They should occur regularly, at a convenient time, in comfortable quarters, with all members notified or reminded in advance. Members should be familiar with the group's constitution or bylaws and its goals and objectives. People who are to give reports should be aware of this and should make provision for substitutes to do so if they must be absent. An agenda must be prepared in advance and distributed to each member either beforehand or upon arrival at the meeting.

Just before the meeting starts it must be determined that a

quorum is present. If a quorum is not present all that should be done is to set a time to reconvene ("fix the time to adjourn") or to recess and try to achieve a quorum. A quorum is the minimum number needed to transact business. Requiring one is a protection for the membership so a very small clique cannot transact business against the majority's wishes. The figure for a necessary quorum varies and should be set realistically in the bylaws. If not so stated, parliamentary law says it is a majority of the entire membership. Voluntary societies should base their quorum on a percentage of members, as large a number of members as can reasonably be depended on to be present at any given meeting. At a mass meeting everyone there constitutes a quorum. At any properly called meeting of an organization where there are no dues, those attending constitute a quorum. At a convention (a body delegate) the quorum is a majority of those registered.

CHAPTER **6**

STRUCTURE OF A MEETING

THE ORDER of business is often stipulated in the bylaws or the standing rules. It is flexible and items can be taken out of order by a two-thirds vote "to suspend the rules." For instance, a club program may be scheduled first to save a busy speaker the necessity of sitting through a lengthy business meeting. Although *Robert's Rules of Order* has a stated order of business which is listed below, it is a matter of procedure not inherent in a club's structure. Guests may be introduced at any logical time after the opening, according to the group's custom. Roll call can be omitted, with sign-up sheets used, or in a small group the secretary can simply note absentees. Opening devotionals, patriotic exercises, and rituals are at the discretion of the group.

Robert's Order for a Meeting

1. Call to order
2. Opening exercises or ceremonies
3. Roll call
4. Reading and approval of minutes
5. Reports of officers, boards, Standing Committees
6. Reports of Special Committees
7. Special Orders
8. Unfinished Business and General Orders
9. New Business

10. Good of the Order
11. Announcements
12. Program
13. Adjournment

The scenario for a meeting can go something like this:

President (lightly taps gavel and members cease talking): "The meeting will please come to order. We will open our meeting with the Pledge of Allegiance."

"The secretary will please read the minutes of the previous meeting."..."Are there any corrections to the minutes? (Slight pause) There being no corrections the minutes are approved as read." If a member speaks out to note an error, the president says, "The secretary will make the correction. Are there any other corrections? (Pause) The minutes are approved as corrected." A majority vote or general consent can postpone reading of the minutes to another meeting.

"The next business in order is hearing reports of officers. The treasurer will now report."..."The report will be filed for audit."

"Has the corresponding secretary a report to make or any communications not requiring action?" Matters which require action should be saved for New Business. Letter reading should be kept to a minimum. The Executive Board can dispose of much correspondence, which can also be summarized, excerpted, and even discarded. Members have the right to know but they should be spared inundation.

"The next business in order is hearing reports of the Executive Board."

"The next business in order is a report from the Standing Committee on...."

"We will now hear the report of the Special Committee appointed at the last meeting to...." A Special Committee ceases when its work is done, with the presentation of its report usually its final act. No motion is needed to dissolve it as it automatically disbands. However, courtesy requires the president to thank the members and acknowledge their work.

Special Orders come here. They constitute an appointment to take up a particular motion. At one meeting a member may move that a resolution be postponed to the next meeting and made a Special Order. This requires a two-thirds vote for passage and is included in the minutes. The president must be familiar with the minutes, for Special Orders automatically come on the agenda before Unfinished Business and General Orders. A Special Order can be specified for a particular time of day, interrupting any business being discussed except for another Special Order set for an earlier hour. No motion to take it up is required. The president simply announces a Special Order, states the motion, and deliberations begin. Nomination and elections can be considered Special Orders without a motion so designating them, so they will be held before other business.

"Unfinished Business is now in order." The president does not ask if there is any Unfinished Business, but makes a point to know whether or not there is. If a motion was under consideration when the last meeting adjourned, it is not dead, just unfinished and should be taken up where it was left off. It is not "old" business any more than a half-baked cake is an old cake.

General Orders are practically indistinguishable from Unfinished Business. They are motions that have been postponed. Unlike Special Orders, General Orders do not have to be specifically named, and they require only a majority vote. The normal motion to postpone creates a General Order. Items can be taken from the table here. Since the president may not know that a motion will be made to take an item from the table, the member making the motion must address the chair quickly here, even interrupting the chair, as she announces the next item of business.

"We are now ready for New Business."

Good of the Order is an item that is optional and can occur when a general discussion is warranted. It is not recorded in the minutes and no motion should be made. Here members can freely express their opinions off the record on matters dealing with the welfare of individual members and the state of the organization.

"Are there any announcements?"

The president never "turns the meeting over" to a program chairman. Rather he says, "Our vice president, Mary Sloan, will now introduce the program."

A meeting can be adjourned by the president with general consent: "If there is no further business, the meeting is adjourned," or "If there is no objection, the meeting will be adjourned." Also, a member may make a motion to adjourn. It is treated as any other motion, requires majority vote for adoption, and after the vote is announced the president says, "The meeting is adjourned."

MAIN MOTIONS

The business of an organization is carried on through Main Motions, whose object is to introduce new business for consideration. While there are a variety of motions, a Main Motion is the lowest in rank so it can be perfected without infringing on the rights of members.

A positive statement is best for a Main Motion as it is then easier to vote on correctly. For instance, a negative motion, such as "I move that the P.T.A. not sponsor a paper drive," requires those in favor of having one to vote no, while those opposing it vote aye, and this can confuse many people. It is permissible for the chair to assist a member in rewording a motion.

While a Main Motion is often made verbally, it is helpful to write it out so it is understandable, the secretary can transcribe it verbatim more easily, and the chair has no difficulty in stating it correctly. If it is a sudden idea and poorly phrased, the chair can help by asking, "Does the member mean...?"

The reason for requiring seconds to motions is to show that at least one person other than the proposer favors the motion. Often a second comes quickly and automatically by someone simply saying, without need to obtain the floor, "I second it." Unless the club wishes it, names of seconders are not ordinarily required to be recorded in the minutes. Only one second is needed for a Main Motion, and in committees and small boards seconds to motions are not required.

Here is a list of motions that do *not* require a second.

Call to Order
Point to Order
Objection to Consideration of a Motion
Question of Privilege
Divide the Question (under certain circumstances)
Division of the House
Withdraw or Modify a Motion
Filling Blanks
Parliamentary Inquiry and Point of Information
Orders of the Day
Requests of any kind
Adjourn

After a motion is made, seconded, and the chair states it, the motion is open to discussion. The discussion is called "debate," and there are some fundamental rules connected with it. The presiding officer lets the introducer of the Main Motion speak first, then tries to call on someone opposed, alternating viewpoints after that if possible. No personal remarks should intrude on debate, and discussion must be kept to the motion at hand. Common courtesy should always prevail. Organizational rules should specify a time limit for debate, unless the usual parliamentary custom prevails. This calls for a ten-minute limit on each speech with a second ten-minute limit for speeches after all that wish have had a chance to speak. Debate can be limited by a Subsidiary Motion. In boards and committee there is no limit of time per speech or the number of times a person may speak, with the president also allowed to speak.

It is rude to call "Question" before all have finished speaking; and, contrary to popular belief, it does not force an immediate vote, as the Main Motion must be adequately debated.

Until the chair states a motion, it belongs to the maker who can change or even withdraw it. Members can also offer changes. However, once the chair formally states it, it belongs to the House and changes and withdrawals must follow accepted procedures. These are discussed under "Amend" or "Withdraw a Motion."

Resolutions are Main Motions more formally stated. Preceded by the word "Resolved" and "That" (with a capital "T"), they often end committee reports and should be written out. The use of "Whereas" as a preamble is now considered obsolete, as the reasons for the resolution are covered in debate.

When discussion lags, the chair should say, "Are you ready for the question? The question is on the motion...." The vote is taken and the result is announced.

It is not usually permissible to reintroduce a motion, or one very similar, at the same meeting. However, a defeated motion may be offered again in the future.

When a Main Motion is before the House, secondary motions may be introduced. These may be renewed because progress in debate changes the situation.

VOTING

A discussion of voting is concerned first with a numerical description and then with the methods of voting. Most decisions in a deliberative body are made by majority vote, meaning more than half of the votes *cast*. People cannot be required to vote if they are in attendance and choose not to vote.

A *plurality* means the greatest number in an election with three or more candidates, so a plurality can be much less than a majority. If four candidates are running and twenty-five votes are cast, the vote count could be seven, six, six, six, so the winner would be declared with only seven votes, or just 28 percent in favor of the winning candidate.

If a motion requires a two-thirds vote for adoption, the president should state it before taking the vote. Unlike a majority vote, which can often be easily determined by the loudness of the "aye's" and "no's," a two-thirds vote must be counted to determine the numerical ratio. Note that though slightly over 66 percent carries in a two-thirds vote, minority rights are protected because just slightly less than one-third can defeat a motion. A two-thirds vote means two-thirds of votes cast, with blank votes never counting. There can be a big difference between two-thirds of votes cast, two-thirds of members present, and two-thirds of the entire membership.

Generally the type of numerical vote that is required for a measure to pass is established to protect fully the rights of members. For instance, unless the bylaws state otherwise, the constitution can be amended at any regular meeting, without previous notice given, by a majority vote of the entire membership, not just of those present. This type of amendment is unlikely to happen, for rarely is everyone in attendance. It can be amended at a regular meeting by a two-thirds vote of those cast if notice was given at the previous meeting, or it can be amended at a special meeting if notice was given and a copy of the proposed amendment was enclosed in the announcement calling the meeting.

By the same token some motions require a two-thirds vote and some a majority (sometimes incorrectly called "a simple majority"). Generally those that limit rights require a two-thirds vote, and those that give or restore them require a majority vote. The following require a two-thirds vote:
- Rescinding/repealing without previous notice
- Relating to nominations
- Consideration of a motion
- Suspending rules
- Limiting or extending limits of debate
- Previous question

Notice that closing nominations requires a two-thirds vote but reopening needs only a majority, again because the first limits members rights and the latter extends them.

There are eight recognized methods of voting: voice, rising (standing), show of hands, ballot, machine, roll call, absentee, and general consent.

Voice vote (*viva voce*) is the simplest and most common, whereby all in favor say aye and those opposed say no. Also frequently used in small groups is the show of hands whereby the chair says, "All those in favor of the motion please raise the right hand." Then, "Please lower your hands and all opposed please raise the right hand." In these votes the chair makes a rough assessment of the outcome by hearing or by sight. If the vote is close or the chair has difficulty calling the vote, a rising vote may be taken.

If a member believes that a mistake has been made in announcing a voice or show of hands vote, the member may ask for a rising vote. Without securing recognition from the chair the member says, "I call for a division." This action must be done before any other business transpires. The chair must then immediately take another vote by saying, "A division has been called. We shall vote again. Those in favor please stand." Then the result is announced, "There are fifteen in the affirmative and thirteen in the negative; the motion is adopted." (Note that the newly revised version of *Robert's Rules of Order* says that calling for a division means calling for a standing vote, and a separate motion is necessary to obtain a counted vote. For most clubs, however, it would seem most practical for the president to count the votes, unless it is obviously unnecessary, since the reason for calling for a division is to get an accurate count.)

A rising vote is always necessary for a two-thirds vote. After a count, the president says, "There are fifteen votes or two-thirds in the affirmative. The motion is adopted." If the vote is close, a member may rise and without waiting to be recognized, say, "I call for a recount." The recount must be done at once.

The president may vote in a show of hands or rising vote when there is a tie or when her vote makes a tie. A tie vote is automatically lost unless the president cares to break it. When the president's vote makes a tie, the motion is lost. In a ballot vote the president may vote during the election but not after the count. Again a tie vote is lost.

The ballot, or secret, vote is taken usually in important elections when members might not want their preferences known. Any piece of paper on which they can write their choices is satisfactory. A tally sheet should be used to record the vote and ballots should be kept until there is no possibility of a recount being requested, then they should be destroyed.

One ballot can be used for all officers on a slate, or a vote may be taken for each office separately, with the result for president announced before voting on a vice president begins and so on.

In large organizations much more stringent rules are required than for small clubs. Ballots are printed; perhaps credentials must be shown before a ballot is given out; one or more ballot boxes are used (checked beforehand to see that they are empty); poll watchers may be required as votes are tallied; and tally sheets must be written in ink and signed by the tellers.

Machines, especially computers, are being used more frequently now because of their speed and accuracy.

The time-consuming roll call vote is used in legislative assemblies where voters represent others who are entitled to know how their representatives voted on issues and candidates.

If the membership is scattered or cannot always be expected to attend the annual meeting (where major elections take place), a system of absentee ballots may be employed. (See illustration 12 on page 81.) Absentee ballots are used by some associations, such as a homeowners group, to decide major issues. Blank ballots are mailed to members along with two envelopes. The member marks the ballot, seals it in the small envelope and then mails it back in the larger. Sometimes such groups make provision for a signed proxy ballot for an election, which can be sent in or given to an authorized proxy. The proxy statement may also authorize someone to vote for a member on matters coming up at the annual meeting.

The use of general consent is a time-saver. It cannot be used to pass a Main Motion, to elect officers, or to decide other important matters. But it is useful for procedures when no opposition is likely. If there is objection, a vote must be taken. It is commonly used in approval of the minutes when the president says, "Are there any corrections?" Silence gives consent, then the president says, "The minutes are approved as read." Before a motion has been stated, the president can say, "If there is no objection, the member making the motion may withdraw it." When debate on a question seems to be over, the president can say, "Is there further discussion?" Silence again indicates the general consent to put the matter to vote. Adjournment frequently takes place this way.

NOMINATION AND ELECTION OF OFFICERS

The method of nominating and electing officers should be prescribed in an organization's constitution or bylaws, usually calling for presentation of a slate by a nominating committee, with nominations then in order from the floor. Use of a nominating ballot can also be designated and can be desirable, as it accurately shows members' preferences. If nomination is by ballot, then normally no candidates are nominated from the floor as each member has already had a chance to present a nominee. Usually clubs declare that the two candidates with the highest number of nominations are the official candidates in the ensuing election, but unless the bylaws so decree, they cannot limit the ballot to the two highest names without a two-thirds vote to do so. Otherwise they would be unduly limiting members' rights.

For the more customary way of working through a nominating committee, the bylaws should spell out the number on the committee and how they are to be chosen. Traditionally the committee is composed of outgoing officers. Long-term members who understand the requirements of the office are also good choices. While some clubs allow the president to appoint the committee as with any other Special Committee, others prefer that the committee be elected by the membership to avoid perpetuation of control.

In preparing its slate, which can have one or two names for

each office as the society prefers, the committee should check first to see if nominees will serve if elected.

The chairman of the Nominating Committee makes a report as any other committee chairman does: "Mister President, the Nominating Committee submits the following names in nomination." As in other committee reports, no second is required as there are several people on the committee endorsing the recommendation. The chair hands the list to the presiding officer, and the committee, having finished its task, is automatically disbanded.

The chair should then inquire if there are further nominations for president. The secretary keeps the list of names placed in nomination from the floor. A member can rise, receive recognition and say, "Madam President, I wish to nominate Louis Edwards for president." No second is required. However, second speeches are permissible and are generally used in very large conventions where the people do not know everyone else. The president announces the name, asks if there are further nominations for president, pauses, and then says, "If not, the nominations are closed." The president then proceeds to ask for further nominations for each additional office.

This closing of nominations by general consent usually works satisfactorily. However, the more formal way may be followed. A vote to close nominations requires a two-thirds vote, as it limits the rights of members. To close, a member rises, and after recognition by the chair, says, "I move that the nominations for president be closed." If this motion is seconded, the chair states it and puts it to a vote immediately, as a motion to close nominations is not debatable. It requires a two-thirds affirmative vote for passage because it is limiting rights of members.

If a member wishes to make a nomination after closure but before the election, she can rise, gain recognition, and say, "I move that the nominations for president be reopened." If this is seconded, the chair states it and puts it to a vote immediately. Because this action is restoring rights of members, only an affirmative majority vote is needed for passage.

When all nominations have been completed, voting takes place. If the bylaws call for a secret ballot for election of officers, it must be done that way. This method is usually preferable as it saves possible embarrassment. A voice vote, show of hands, or standing vote can be taken, and the president calls out the names for voting in the order that they were placed in nomination.

Unless otherwise stated in the constitution or bylaws, a majority vote is required for election. Seldom is a two-thirds vote required. Many bylaws stipulate a plurality because voting must continue until a majority is received by a candidate for each office. This process could take a long time, continuing through many ballotings. If there is nothing said about numbers in the bylaws, a motion may be passed before the election stipulating whether a majority or plurality will be required. In a majority election, held by voice or visible means, there is no need to continue voting after one person receives a majority. If forty members are present and the first candidate receives twenty-one votes, that person has the majority and is automatically elected.

If there is only one candidate for each office on a slate and the bylaws permit it, at the close of nominations the chair can say, "If there is no objection the candidates will be elected." (Pause). "Since there is no objection, the candidates are elected." This election is by general consent.

Sometimes a misguided person rises and makes a motion that an officer be elected by acclamation. This effort shows confusion on the part of the person making the motion. In the first place "acclamation" does not mean "unanimously" but means "by voice," which is usually not the intent at all.

Also, the motion is unnecessary, because if only one name has been suggested for the office, the chair may proceed without a motion from the floor. In addition, it is a double motion, for to close nomination requires a two-thirds vote and to elect requires a majority. Also a two-thirds vote must always be a counted one. If it is an attempt to shut out other nominations, it is totally out of order. The chair should deal with this situation tactfully if it is a simple error. However, if the motion is made in malice and the chair does not declare it out of order, a member may rise to a Point of Order and insist on the right of nomination.

The practice of having the secretary cast an elective ballot is out of order if the constitution states that election of officers shall be by ballot. A clause, however, can be inserted in the constitution to say that if there is only one candidate for an office, the secretary may cast the elective ballot. The secretary should then write the name of the candidate on a blank piece of paper, hand it to the president, and say, "I hereby cast the ballot of this organization for Cynthia Askew for treasurer." The president then says, "The elective ballot has been cast for Cynthia Askew for treasurer. The chair declares Ms. Askew elected."

In elections of stock corporations and conventions as well as of political parties, there are well-defined methods of nomination and election that differ from those of small clubs. Each club should follow a plan that best suits its needs.

Illustration 12
PROXY BALLOT

ABSENTEE BALLOT PLEASANT VALLEY ESTATES
1985
IMPORTANT NOTE: This ballot is for absentee voting
only. Regular ballots will be available at the annual meeting.

Nominees   Vote for one Nominee

Judy Warren   ☐
1028 Edgewood

Jeffrey Wright   ☐
1903 Smithfield

CHAPTER 7

FIVE CLASSES OF MOTIONS

MOTIONS ARE divided into five classes: Main, Privileged, Subsidiary, Incidental, and Unclassified or Miscellaneous. (See charts on pages 111-116.) A Main Motion is the raw material of the club's business. Subsidiary Motions help refine it and bring it to completion. Incidental Motions are lesser tools that do this also, and Privileged Motions deal with emergencies.

MAIN MOTION

While there can never be more than one Main Motion before the assembly at any given time, Secondary Motions may be made to aid its passage. Then the Subsidiary Motion replaces the Main Motion and becomes the currently pending question. A question can arise that is incidental and interrupts the pending question. Then the Incidental Motion becomes the immediately pending question until it is disposed. Privileged Motions may be made that override all other matters, even a motion to adjourn.

The Main Motion, the five Privileged, and the seven Subsidiary Motions form a thirteen-rank hierarchy called "order of precedence." In the chart at the end of this section the highest ranking appears first and the lowest at the bottom. While a motion is pending, those ranked above it are in order and those listed below it are out of order. Incidental, Unclassified, and Miscellaneous Motions are nonranking among themselves. Their order depends upon necessity at the time presented.

For each motion one must keep in mind eight points:
- What is its purpose?
- Is it debatable?
- Is it amendable?
- To what motions does it yield?
- What vote is necessary to adopt it?
- May it be reconsidered?
- What is the proper language that must be used to make it?

PRIVILEGED MOTIONS

The five Privileged Motions in order of precedence are:
1. Fix the Time to Adjourn
2. Adjourn
3. Recess
4. Question of Privilege
5. Orders of the Day

Since Privileged Motions deal with emergencies, they take precedence over all pending questions, and they are undebatable; a vote must be taken on them without discussion. Subsidiary Motions cannot be attached to them except the Motion To Amend, which may be applied to Fix the Time to Adjourn and To Take a Recess. Privileged Motions may be made while a subject is pending. The first three on the list above, if made while no business is pending, become Incidental Main Motions so then they are debatable and amendable.

Fix the Time to Adjourn

Purpose: to set time to continue meeting.

Requires a second.

Not debatable (when privileged).

May be amended as to time and place.

Yields to appropriate Incidental Motions and To Reconsider.

Majority vote required.

May be reconsidered.

Form: "I move that when we adjourn, we adjourn to meet (at 3:00 P.M. tomorrow).

This motion is very useful if some business must be completed at a certain meeting, yet the hour grows late. It has the effect of dividing one meeting into two parts.

It can be made when business is pending but not when someone has the floor. If made when no other business is pending, it is an Incidental Main Motion, not Privileged, is debatable and amendable, and may have a Subsidiary Motion attached to it. It can be made even after the group has voted to adjourn so long as the presider has not declared the meeting adjourned, but it should be made sooner.

Adjourn

Purpose: to end the meeting.

Second required.

Not debatable.

Not amendable.

Yields to one Privileged Motion, appropriate Incidental motions, and To Reconsider.

Majority vote required.

May not be reconsidered.

Form: "I move that we adjourn."

Since this motion is the second highest in rank, it may be made while any motion is pending except the one that outranks it—"To Fix the Time to Adjourn." Before putting this motion to vote it is the duty of the president to remind members if any important business must yet be decided at that meeting. This reminder allows the person making the motion to withdraw it. After the vote the meeting is still in session until the president actually says, "The meeting is adjourned," so announcements and other important statements can still be made. Business on the floor when the meeting was adjourned is taken up at the next meeting as unfinished business, beginning at the point where it was when adjournment came.

Meetings may also be adjourned by general consent.

Adjournment *sine die* (without a day) closes a legislative session and dissolves the assembly if no other meeting has been set.

Recess

Purpose: to provide an intermission, for rest, meals, counting ballots, etc.

Second required.

Not debatable.

Is amendable to stipulate a time.

Yields to two higher ranking Privileged Motions, appropriate Incidentals, and To Reconsider.

Majority vote required.

Cannot be reconsidered.

Form: "I move that we have a ten-minute recess."

At meetings that last a long time it is necessary to recess at intervals, although a speaker should not be interrupted. If the length of time needed for the recess cannot be foreseen, such as for counting ballots, the motion can be, "I move that we recess until the call of the chair." Upon return from recess the meeting resumes deliberation as though there had been no interruption.

A recess may be taken by common consent.

Question of Privilege

Purpose: to obtain action immediately in an emergency.
No second required.
Not debatable.
Not amendable.
Yields to higher motions, appropriate Incidentals.
Form: "I rise to a question of privilege."

A member may rise even though the floor has been assigned to another and may, if it is sufficiently urgent, interrupt a speech. The problem may be that the room is too hot or too cold, there is noise that prevents hearing, the loudspeaker system is faulty, or some other similar interference with a member's rights. The difficulty should be corrected at once.

A member may also rise on a Question of Personal Privilege.

Member: "Mister President, I rise to a question of personal privilege."

President: "State your question."

Member: "I don't have any agenda. Are there more copies?"

The president sees that the person gets an agenda if one is available.

If two questions are raised at the same time, the one affecting all the members is attended to before that of one member.

Orders of the Day

Purpose: to demand that the group conform to the agenda.
No second required.
Not debatable.
Not amendable.
Yields to higher ranking motions, appropriate Incidentals, and the motion To Reconsider.

Two-thirds negative vote required *not* to return to the regular orders.

Form: "I call for the orders of the day."

This can be moved by any member without rising or being recognized even if it interrupts discussion on the floor. It is the duty of the president to announce business to come before the group and to keep the group on track. If she does her job well, there is never any need for this motion. Once Orders of the Day are called for, the presiding officer must immediately proceed with the agenda unless the group by common consent or a two-thirds vote agrees to do otherwise.

Sometimes it is used as a reminder of a Special Order which the chair has forgotten.

SUBSIDIARY MOTIONS

As has been stated, a Main Motion introduces the business of an assembly and Subsidiary Motions help that business along to completion. They must pertain to the Main Motion that is pending and serve to help dispose of it. Since only one Main Motion can be on the floor at a time, without them the House would have to approve or defeat each motion exactly as originally stated by the chair, and no other Main Motion could be introduced until the preceding had been disposed of. Therefore subsidiary motions can be thought of as time savers as well as expediters.

No Subsidiary Motion can be made while another member has the floor. All must be seconded. Five require a majority vote and two, a two-thirds vote.

In rank Subsidiary Motions come after Privileged Motions, the highest ranking of all because they are concerned with protecting the rights of members.

To smooth the process of the business at hand, the seven Subsidiary Motions have their own order of precedence. The

list below shows this order, with the highest rank at the top.
1. Lay a Question on the Table
2. Previous Question
3. Limit or Extend Limits of Debate
4. Postpone Definitely
5. Commit or Recommit
6. Amend
7. Postpone Indefinitely

Lay a Question on the Table (To Table)

Purpose: to postpone for more pressing business or to delay action until a more favorable time.

Second required.

Not debatable.

Not amendable.

Yields to Privileged Motions and appropriate Incidentals.

Majority vote required.

May not be reconsidered, but when a question is tabled, it may be taken from the table later.

Form: "I move to table the motion."

The intent of this motion is not to kill it, as the lowest ranking Postpone Indefinitely can be used. It simply stops debate and amendments in order to postpone temporarily. A question remains on the table until the end of the next session unless it is taken up before that time. It can be taken from the table by majority vote at the same session, provided another item of business is transacted after it was tabled. If not taken from the table before the end of the next meeting, it ceases to exist. If the motion To Table does not carry, members continue to discuss the subject as though the motion had not been made.

Previous Question

Purpose: to stop debate and bring the pending question to vote.

Second required.

Not debatable.

Not amendable.

Yields to higher ranking motions and motion To Reconsider.

Two-thirds vote required.

May be reconsidered.

Form: "I move the previous question (meaning the main motion)."

The term for this motion is a seventeenth-century one and can be misleading. It simply means to stop talking about the motion and vote on it. When this motion is approved, all discussion, including making amendments, ceases and the chair puts the main motion to vote. If it fails to carry, the original motion is still open for debate.

The common practice of calling out "Question" is rude and does not stop debate.

Limit or Extend Limits of Debate

Purpose: to regulate debate.

Second required.

Not debatable.

Is amendable.

Yields to higher ranking motions, appropriate Incidentals, and motion To Reconsider.

Two-thirds vote required.

May be reconsidered even though partially executed.

Form: "I move that debate be limited to three minutes," or "I move that debate be extended on this motion to three persons with fifteen-minute speeches."

In parliamentary law members are allowed one ten-minute speech on each motion and a second ten-minute speech after all wishing to speak have done so. This motion allows the assembly, because of the nature of the subject, to make additional time for longer speeches, or to allow for more than the two speeches, or to decrease the length and number of speeches allowed.

When this motion is adopted limiting debate, it applies to any new amendment or other interrupting motion while the order is in force. An extension of debate applies only to the question specified. The changes in debate rules are in force only for the session at which they were made.

Postpone Definitely

Purpose: to delay action to a specific time.
Second required.
Is debatable.
Amendable by altering the time or to make it a Special Order.
Yields to higher ranking motions, appropriate Incidentals, To Amend, To Reconsider.
Majority vote required. When it is a Main Motion or is used to make a Special Order, it requires a two-thirds vote.
May be reconsidered.
Form: "I move to postpone action on this matter to our next meeting," or "I move to postpone consideration of this matter until three o'clock."

This motion is useful if the meeting is running too long, a question needs further reflection or if a group of members wants time to gather strength for its side. It is proper to delay to the next meeting; it then automatically comes up when Unfinished Business is in order. When the motion is made, seconded, and stated by the chair, debate may be on the merits of postponing but not on the motion itself.

If a member says, "I move the motion be postponed and made a Special Order for next meeting (or for 7:40 P.M. at the next meeting), it then comes before Unfinished Business if the time arrives before then. Since it interrupts rights of members in this case, a two-thirds vote is required.

Commit or Recommit (To Refer to Committee)

Purpose: to place a question temporarily in the hands of a committee to investigate, recommend, or take action.

Second required.

Debatable only as to advisability of referring to committee and to which committee.

Is Amendable.

Majority vote required.

May be reconsidered.

Form: "I move that we refer this matter to the Buildings and Grounds Committee," or "I move that we refer this question to a committee of five appointed by the chair with instructions to report at the next meeting."

Business that cannot be acted on immediately can be referred to an appropriate Standing Committee, or a Special Committee can be formed to handle it.

Sometimes bylaws stipulate that the president may appoint Special Committees, and provision is made to suspend the rules to allow a president *pro tem* to make Special Committee appointments. If this is not in the bylaws, then action to commit must include how the Special Committee is to be selected.

The chair may appoint a committee by common consent or, after the motion To Commit is made, can ask, "How shall the committee be appointed?" Without rising a member may say, "Appointed by the chair," or "By nominations from the floor," or "Nominated by the chair." Appropriate action is then taken immediately.

The committee formed takes with it all motions and amendments relating to the matter that have been previously made, and further action by the House on the matter should not be taken until the committee reports.

It is possible for the entire group to act as a committee. In a very large group this is called going into the "committee of the whole." In a small group the motion is made that the question "be considered informally." Upon seconding and majority approval, the group can then discuss with no limit on debate. The presiding officer acts as chair and motions are recorded in the minutes. No motion is needed to end informal discussion as it is automatically over when the question under discussion is disposed of.

Amend

Purpose: to change or modify.
Second required.
Debatable but debate must be confined to merits of amendment.
May be amended by an amendment of the second degree.
Yields to higher ranking motions.
Majority vote required for pending action. Two-thirds vote required to amend something previously adopted, such as a constitution or bylaws because it then becomes a Main Motion, not a Subsidiary one.
May be reconsidered.
Form: 'I move to amend the motion by."
When a motion is made, the need to alter it may be apparent at once or come later as a result of discussion. Amendments must be directly related to their Main Motion and must be voted on first before the motion as amended is voted on. After a Main Motion has been stated by the chair, it may be amended in one of five ways:

1. By striking out one or more consecutive words
2. By inserting one or more consecutive words
3. By striking out one or more consecutive words and substituting others in their place
4. By adding one or more words to the end of the motion

5. By substituting a New Motion

A member rises, addresses the presider, and is recognized. The member then states the proposed amendment which must be seconded (the seconder need not rise or be recognized.) Then the presider states the amendment, calls for discussion, and then takes the vote and announces the result. If the amendment is lost, the vote is then taken on the motion as originally made.

It is permissible for the person who made the original motion to simply "accept the amendment." Then, after inquiring if there is any objection and if there is none, the presider can declare the motion amended. The question then is on adoption of the amended motion.

An amendment to a Main Motion is a primary amendment. An amendment to an amendment is secondary. A secondary motion must be acted on before the primary one, which in turn precedes action on the original motion.

To amend by substitution is in order only when an entire section, paragraph, or resolution is to be changed. In this case the original paragraph is open to amendment first: "It is moved and seconded that the first paragraph be amended by substituting this paragraph. (Read substitution) Are there amendments to the paragraph to be removed? (Pause) If there are none, are there amendments to the proposed paragraph? (Pause) If not, the question is on substituting the proposed paragraph for the pending one." If this motion carries, the presider says, "The question is now on adoption of the resolution as amended, which reads '....' Are you ready for the question?"

A proposed amendment to the constitution or bylaws is a Main Motion because the constitution or bylaws have already been adopted. Therefore a proposed amendment to an amendment is a primary one.

Related to the amendment process is the procedure known

as "Filling Blanks," which can save much time when names, places, and amounts of money must be included in a motion. For example, a motion might be made to spend five hundred dollars on repairs to a building. If another member thinks a different amount would be better, he can move "to create a blank by striking out the sum of five hundred dollars." After it is seconded and approved by majority vote, the members suggest other amounts, which are then voted on until one receives a majority. Then the Main Motion is acted on. A motion may be made with a blank in it, or the chair may ask for general consent to create a blank in a motion that has been made.

The following list of motions cannot be amended:

Lay a Question on the Table
Nominate officers, committee members, etc.
Adjourn (when Privileged)
Amend a Secondary Amendment
Postpone Indefinitely
Reconsider
Point of Order
Question of Privilege
Take from the Table
Suspend a Rule
Take up a Question out of its Proper Order
Withdraw or Modify a Motion
Permission to Read Papers
Permission to Continue Speaking after Indecorum Called
Appeal from the Decision of the Chair
Call to Order
Orders of the Day
Objection to Consideration of a Motion
Parliamentary Inquiry and Point of Information
Division of the House

Motion to Reconsider
Request of any Kind
Previous Question

Postpone Indefinitely

Purpose: to kill a motion without bringing it to a vote.
Second required.
Debatable, and merits of Main Motion may be debated.
Not amendable.
Affirmative vote may be reconsidered.
Majority vote required.
Yields to all motions except Main Motion.
Form: "I move the matter be postponed indefinitely."

As the lowest ranking motion, next to the Main Motion, an indefinite postponement can be offered only if nothing else is pending. While its stated purpose is to remove the subject from that meeting, its end result is usually to dispose of the Main Motion without bringing it to a vote, since for all practical purposes it kills the motion. Sometimes it is a way to test the strength of the Main Motion, for if it carries it is obvious the Main Motion will be lost. While the Main Motion then cannot be reintroduced at the same meeting, it can be brought before the group at another meeting. At other times this motion is made when members have used up their alloted time to speak, for it allows them to debate the issues of the Main Motion again while discussing whether to postpone it indefinitely or not.

Main Motion

Purpose: to introduce new business.
Second required.
Is debatable.
Always amendable.
Yields to all higher ranking motions, appropriate Inciden-

tals, and motion To Reconsider.

Majority vote required.

May be reconsidered.

Form: "I move that...." or "I move to...."

The Main Motion, which introduces a subject to the assembly, is the lowest in order of precedence because it is just that, the "bottom line" at a meeting. All Subsidiary Motions are designed to help refine it or to expedite proper disposal of it. Only one Main Motion can be before the House at a time and all Subsidiary Motions arising from it must be disposed of temporarily or permanently before it can be voted on. The person who introduces the Main Motion is entitled to speak on its behalf first and last in debate.

Although there is a group of motions called "Incidental Motions," which arise out of the business at hand, there is also a group called "Incidental Main Motions," which can be made when no other business is pending. Unlike regular Main Motions, they do not introduce new business but are concerned only with procedure. These include To Fix the Time to Adjourn and To Adjourn, when they are not privileged; To Adjourn, To Recess, To Amend Something Previously Adopted, and To Refer to Committee, which can be made while a Main Motion is pending. They hold over other motions out of which they grow because they are timely, apt, or appropriate.

INCIDENTAL MOTIONS

Most Incidental Motions develop out of the business being done, and they have no order of precedence among themselves. However, they must be decided on before the question on which they arise is decided and before additional business is taken up, so they take precedence over the pending question.

Here is a list of Incidental Motions:

Point of Order
Appeal
Suspend a Rule (two-thirds vote required)
Objection to Consideration of a Motion (two-thirds vote)
Divide the Question
Consideration by Paragraph (Seriatim)
Division of the Group
Relating to Nominations
Motions Pertaining to Voting
Requests Growing out of Pending Business, such as Parliamentary Inquiry and Point of Information
Withdraw or Modify a Motion
Read Papers
Excused from a Duty
Request for any other Privilege

Point of Order

Purpose: to enforce the rules.

No second required.

Not debatable but chair can consult an authority.

Not amendable.

Yields to Privileged Motions and To Table.

Chair usually decides but requires majority vote if submitted to the group.

May not be reconsidered.

Form: "I rise to a point of order."

It is the duty of the chair to enforce the rules of proper parliamentary procedure, tactfully and courteously correcting violations of it. It is also the right of any member to insist that the rules be followed. A member, upon observing a violation that is not corrected, rises without waiting for recognition and says, "Mister President, I rise to a point of order." The president replies, "State your point." Then the member explains his complaint, such as, "The motion to suspend the rules requires a two-thirds vote," and then he resumes his seat. The president should reply, "The speaker is correct. The motion does require a two-thirds vote. The motion is lost."

Point of Order may also be raised to stop discourteous conduct.

Appeal

Purpose: to reverse the decision of the chair.
Second required.
Debatable, except under special circumstances.
Not amendable, except under certain circumstances.
Yields to Privileged Motions, To Table, to Reconsider.
When debatable yields to Modify Debate, Previous Question, To Postpone.
Majority negative vote reverses decision of chair.
May be reconsidered.
Form: "I appeal from the decision of the chair." (State appeal.)

Appeals frequently result from a member's rising to a Point of Order. When someone disagrees with the decision of the chair, he may appeal, but the appeal must be made immediately following the ruling. After the member states his appeal, the presiding officer gives her reasons for making the decision. She may then call for a vote, "Those who agree with the decision of the chair say aye." "Those opposed no." If the majority votes in the negative, the decision of the chair is reversed. A tie vote sustains the chair because of the rule that a motion is automatically lost in case of a tie. In this case the motion to overrule is lost, so the decision of the chair is sustained.

While an appeal requires a second in formal proceedings,

in practical application it is seldom required. Appeals and Points of Order are recorded in the minutes.

An appeal is debatable except when it applies to bad conduct or breaking rules of debate or Order of Business. When it is debated members may speak only once and the chair twice, at the beginning to state reasons for the decision and at the end to answer arguments raised in the debate.

Suspend a Rule

Purpose: to allow action contrary to the rules.

Second required.

Not debatable.

Not amendable.

Yields to Privilege (except Orders of the Day, To Table, appropriate Incidentals and To Reconsider).

Two-thirds vote required except a majority in case of a Standing Rule.

May not be reconsidered.

Form: "I move to suspend the rules in order to allow...."

Sometimes it is necessary to suspend rules. For instance, a major conflict may require changing a regular meeting day. If the meeting day is stipulated in a Standing Rule, a majority vote is required to make such an exception. However, a change in Orders of the Day requires a two-thirds vote as it interferes with rights of members. Rules contained in the by-laws cannot be suspended.

A blanket motion to suspend the rules cannot be made; the motion should be specific and never should be done recklessly.

Objection to Consideration of a Motion

Purpose: to avoid discussion of a question that is irrelevant, contentious, unprofitable, or objectionable.

No second required.

Not debatable.
Not amendable.
Yields to Privileges, appropriate Incidentals, To Reconsider.
Two-thirds negative vote required to sustain the objection. Negative vote only may be considered
Form: "I object to the consideration of this motion."

Sometimes a motion is potentially embarrassing or awkward. It can be handled by To Postpone Indefinitely but usually it is better not to wait until discussion has begun but to offer this motion before debate starts. If necessary this motion to object can interrupt a member on the floor.

Divide the Question

Purpose: to consider one subject at a time.
No second required.
Not debatable.
Is amendable.
Yields to all ranking motions except Postpone Indefinitely, To Amend, and yields to appropriate Incidental Motions.
Majority vote required.
May not be reconsidered.
Form: "I move to divide the question."

Applied only to Main Motions and amendments, this motion should be made as soon as the question is introduced. Sometimes a motion is made that has several parts, and it is better to consider them separately. The motion should state how the division is to be made, and after division each part becomes a Main Motion being voted on in the order in which it was stated. Motions can be divided by general consent.

Consideration by Paragraph (Seriatim)

Purpose: to perfect each paragraph before voting.
Second required.

Not debatable.

Not amendable.

Yields to ranking motions higher than Postpone Indefinitely (except To Amend) and to appropriate Incidentals

Majority vote required.

May not be reconsidered.

Form: "I move to consider the question seriatim."

This is used for consideration of a lengthy subject consisting of several sections or paragraphs, such as a constitution or bylaws, or long resolution. To divide the question breaks a motion into distinct parts. This motion, however, is used when all the parts of the resolution or document are closely interrelated and a change in one part could affect other parts. In this procedure, a paragraph or section or series of resolutions is read, debated, and amendments offered with no vote taken on each one. After it has been considered in its entirety, it is open for additional amendments or to have new paragraphs added. Consideration of the preamble comes last, as changes in content may cause the wording of the preamble to change. The vote is then taken on the entire document as amended.

Division of the Group

Purpose: to verify accuracy of an announced vote.

No second required.

Not debatable.

Not amendable.

No motions hold over it.

No vote needed to order a standing vote but a majority needed to order a counted vote.

May not be reconsidered.

Form: "I call for a division of the Group."

The most common method of voting is by voice, which is totally different from a roll call vote where each name is called and the member votes yea or nay. In a voice vote all in the affirmative say aye and those opposed say no. A show of hands is another popular way to vote in small clubs. If the vote is close, however, the chair may not be able to tell the outcome easily. Then she can call for a standing vote. Even this may be hard to call, so the chair then asks members to stand for a counted vote. As each person is counted he should sit.

If there is any doubt about the accuracy of a vote and the chair does not take a standing vote, any member, without rising, can call for a "division." Then the chair takes the vote again by asking the members to stand. The call should come immediately after the doubtful call was made and does not imply that the chair was in error, but that the member who made the call wants to verify the count.

Relating to Nominations

Purpose: to prevent additional nominations.
Second required.
Not debatable.
Not amendable.
Yields to Privileged Motions, appropriate Incidentals, To Reconsider.
Two-thirds vote required for this motion.
May not be reconsidered.
Form: "I move that nominations be closed."

Notice that a two-thirds vote is required if this is a formal motion. However, nominations may be closed by general consent. The president declares the nominations closed after inquiring if there are further nominations. They may be reopened by majority vote.

Motions To Reopen or Close the Polls are similar to closing nominations and are applicable when voting is done by ballot. To Close the Polls means that voting shall cease. Usually the presiding officer simply closes them when all members have voted. If some members arrive after the polls close, it is proper for a motion to be made to reopen them for a certain length of time, such as five minutes, to allow the latecomers to vote. After that time, the chair can declare the polls again closed by general consent.

Parliamentary Inquiry and Point of Information

If a member needs information on correct parliamentary procedure, he rises and says, "Madam President, I rise to a parliamentary inquiry." The president asks the member to state the inquiry, then the president answers the question or asks the parliamentarian to do so. Point of Information is similar except it does not pertain to parliamentary procedure but might concern clarification of a matter under discussion. In this case the member says, "I rise for information."

Since it is not permissible for members to address each other in debate, questions for a speaker must go through the chair: "Mister President, I should like to ask the speaker a question." The president then turns to the speaker who may decline to answer the question (perhaps because the time spent in answering is deducted from the allotted speaking time.) If the speaker consents, the president asks the member to state the question, which must be in the third person and addressed to the chair. The answer should also be addressed to the chair.

Neither Parliamentary Inquiry nor Point of Information needs seconds or voting on.

Withdraw or Modify a Motion

Form: "I request permission to withdraw my motion."

The person making a motion may withdraw it or modify it without anyone's consent before it is stated by the chair. A seconder can withdraw the second if the motion is modified after the second. However, once the motion is stated by the chair, it belongs to the assembly and the maker can withdraw or modify it only with the consent of the assembly.

Permission is usually granted informally, and the chair announces the motion is withdrawn. However, if there is objection to a motion's being withdrawn, the matter must be brought to a vote. When a motion is withdrawn it has the same effect as though it had never been made. It is not necessary to second the motion.

If a motion is made by one member and another wishes it to be withdrawn (perhaps to allow for consideration of more urgent business), the one who wishes the withdrawal rises and without waiting for recognition says, "Madam President, I would like to ask that the motion be withdrawn because...." If the maker agrees, the presiding officer announces the motion is withdrawn.

Read Papers

Reading from books and other written materials must be approved by the assembly before being read. Usually this approval is reached by general consent. Member: "If there is no objection I should like to...." If there is objection the chair must put it to vote with a majority required for passage.

Excused from a Duty

An officer who must give up a position should write a letter of resignation which is then read and a vote taken on acceptance. A member who cannot perform an assignment should make the fact known to the president, who should relieve the member of the obligation.

UNCLASSIFIED OR MISCELLANEOUS MOTIONS

The first five of the motions being considered here bring a question before the assembly again, so they can be called Restoratory Motions.

Take from Table

Purpose: to bring up for debate a motion previously tabled.
Second required.
Not debatable.
Not amendable.
Yields to Privileged Motions, appropriate Incidentals, To Reconsider.
Majority vote required.
May not be reconsidered.
Form: "I move the motion (state) be taken from the table."

Any member, regardless of how he voted to lay a motion on the table, may request it be taken from the table. This motion may be made as soon as the business for which it was laid on the table has been completed, or when unfinished or new business is in order. If the motion To Take from Table is lost, it may be renewed later in the meeting. If this motion is adopted, the chair states the question, and consideration starts up at the point where it stopped earlier.

If a question that has been laid on the table is not taken up at the same meeting or at the next one, it automatically dies, but it can be reintroduced as a new motion later.

Since a motion that is laid on the table can be taken from the table, a better way to kill a Main Motion is to Postpone Indefinitely.

Reconsider

Purpose: to try to secure a new vote.
Second required.
Is debatable.
Not amendable.
Yields to Privileged Motions, appropriate Incidentals, and the four highest Subsidiary Motions.
Majority vote required.
May not be reconsidered.

Form: "I move to reconsider the vote taken on the motion relating....I voted for the motion."

If a motion has been adopted or rejected or postponed indefinitely it can be reconsidered only by passage of a motion To Reconsider, which is the way to rectify hasty, ill-advised action. The motion can be made only by one who voted on the prevailing side and may be made only on the same day or the following calendar day as the vote that is being reconsidered was taken. (Sundays and legal holidays or a recess of a day are not counted.)

If a member is opposed to a motion that appears about to pass, he can vote on the prevailing side so he becomes eligible to call for reconsideration, possibly being able to muster enough opposition to defeat it when it comes before the group again.

Unlike motions to Rescind or Amend Something Previously Adopted, this motion does not propose a reversal of action; it simply proposes a review and the earlier decision may still stand.

If necessary, the motion to reconsider can be made when another question is on the floor, but consideration of the motion thus restored must wait until the interrupted business is concluded.

In committee any member may make a motion To Reconsider and there is no time limitation, but obviously it cannot be done if action required by the motion has already taken place.

The motion To Reconsider requires only a majority vote even though the action being considered requires a two-thirds vote.

Reconsider and Enter on Minutes

This procedure is similar to that of To Reconsider except final action on it cannot be taken until the next regular meeting after the original motion. If it is not called up at that meeting, it dies. This motion can prevent a group that is a temporary majority from taking action which the real majority of the organization would oppose.

The motion must be made by one who voted on the prevailing side.

Rescind

Purpose: to void or repeal action of the past.

Second required.

Is debatable.

May be amended.

Majority vote required with previous notice, two-thirds without notice; rescinding bylaws requires two-thirds.

Affirmative vote may not be reconsidered.

Form: "I move that we rescind the motion (state) which was passed (date)."

This motion is also known as Repeal or Annul. It is a Main Motion and may be made by any member if no business is pending. There are some actions that cannot be rescinded. For instance, if money has already been spent, it cannot be retrieved.

Rescinding is similar to Amend Something Previously Adopted, except amending does not reverse or change the whole previous action, just part of it. Bylaws usually require notice for amendment, and previous notice should also be given if rescinding a past action is likely to have serious opposition. If previous notice is given, a majority of those present can approve it; otherwise a two-thirds vote is needed.

Notice To Rescind may be given at the previous meeting or in a call for a meeting.

Expunge

Where there is vehement disapproval of a previous action, the assembly may vote to expunge the motion or resolution from the records. Since the minutes cannot be obliterated, this is done by drawing a line through the words, then writing "Rescinded and ordered expunged," along with the date when so ordered. The action is then no longer in effect. If the minutes are published, the expunged section is not included. Expunging should be done by the secretary in the presence of the members. A majority vote is necessary.

This procedure is used rarely and is not recommended. A better way to rectify a past mistake is To Rescind the motion if possible or to adopt a resolution disavowing the action.

Ratify

Purpose: to approve and make valid action already taken.
Second required.
Is debatable and opens the main question for discussion.
May be amended.
Majority vote required.
May be reconsidered.
Form: "I move that…"

When adopted, this motion serves to legalize something the officers or the assembly has already done. For instance, occasionally it is necessary for a committee or officers to act in haste, possibly exceeding their authority, but trusting that the group will approve the action. Perhaps bad weather prevented presence of a quorum at a meeting when some business had to be transacted. To ratify action taken at that time, someone simply announces what happened and moves that it be ratified.

MOTIONS THAT ARE IN ORDER WHEN ANOTHER HAS THE FLOOR

Appeal
Call to Order

Orders of the Day
Division of the Group
Objection to Consideration of a Motion
Parliamentary Inquiry
Point of Order
Question of Privilege
Reconsider
Request of any Kind

MOTIONS THAT ARE ALWAYS OUT OF ORDER

Motions not germane to the Main Motion.

Motions renewed at the same meeting.

Motions in violation of federal, state, or local law.

Motions beyond the scope and purpose of the organization.

Dilatory Motions: those that obstruct or confuse the business of the meeting.

Abuse of motions, such as To Reconsider and Point of Order.

A member is never out of order, but a motion may be. The chair has the duty to see that the assembly is not victimized by excesses of members who wish to "show off" their knowledge of parliamentary procedure or who deliberately hamper conduct of business.

The study of parliamentary procedure is a study fascinating for its logic and respect for human rights, and the more facile officers and members become in it, the smoother their organizations run. After mastering the rudiments given here they may wish to advance further by delving into the full authority of *Robert's Rules of Order, Newly Revised,* where procedures are spelled out in greater detail. Conversely, clubs that ignore standard parliamentary practice soon realize how correct Henry M. Robert was when he said, "Where there is no law, but every man does what is right in his own eyes, there is the least of real liberty."

SIMPLIFIED CHART OF MOTIONS

Privileged Motions

Motion	Second Required	Debatable	Amendable	Vote Required	Reconsider	Interrupt Speaker	Purpose	Form
1. Fix the Time to Adjourn	yes	no	yes	majority	yes	no	To set time to continue meeting	"I move that we adjourn to meet at…"
2. Adjourn	yes	no	no	majority	no	no	To end the meeting	"I move that we adjourn."
3. Recess	yes	no	yes	majority	no	no	To provide an intermission	"I move a ten-minute recess."
4. Question of Privilege	no	no	no	none	no	yes	To obtain action immediately in an emergency	"I rise to a question of privilege."
5. Orders of the Day	no	no	no	none[1]	no	yes	To demand the group conform to the agenda	"I call for the orders of the day."

Subsidiary Motions

Motion	Second Required	Debatable	Amendable	Vote Required	Reconsider	Interrupt Speaker	Purpose	Form
6. Lay a Question on the Table	yes	no	no	majority	no	no	To postpone for more pressing business	"I move to table the motion."
7. Previous Question	yes	no	no	$\frac{2}{3}$	yes[2]	no	To stop debate	"I move the previous question."
8. Limit or Extend Limits of Debate	yes	no	yes	$\frac{2}{3}$	yes	no	To regulate debate	"I move that debate be limited to...."
9. Postpone Definitely	yes	yes	yes	majority	yes	no	To delay action to a specific time	"I move to postpone action to..."
10. Commit or Recommit	yes	yes	yes	majority	yes	no	To place question in the hands of a committee	"I move that we refer this matter to...."

Motion	Second Required	Debatable	Amendable	Vote Required	Reconsider	Interrupt Speaker	Purpose	Form
11. Amend*	yes	yes	yes	majority	yes	no	To change or modify	"I move to amend by...."
12. Postpone Indefinitely	yes	yes	no	majority	yes	no	To kill a motion without bringing it to a vote	"I move the matter be postponed."
13. Main Motion	yes	yes	yes	majority	yes	no	To introduce new business	"I move that...."

Privileged Motions take precedence over Subsidiary Motions. Rank is in descending order high to low.

[1]Must be enforced on demand unless set aside by ⅔ vote

[2]If vote was affirmative, only before any vote taken under it

*Sometimes a Main Motion, requiring ⅔ vote

Incidental Motions

Motion	Second Required	Debatable	Amendable	Vote Required	Reconsider	Interrupt Speaker	Purpose	Form
Point of Order	no	no	no	none	no	yes	To enforce the rules	"I rise to a point of order."
Appeal	yes	yes	no	majority negative	yes	yes	To reverse the decision of the chair	"I appeal from the decision of the chair."
Suspend a Rule	yes	no	no	⅔	no	no	To allow action contrary to the rules	"I move to suspend the rules."
Objection to Consideration of a Motion	no	no	no	⅔ negative	negative only	yes	To avoid discussion of a question	"I object to the consideration of this motion."
Divide the Question	no	no	yes	majority	no	no	To consider one thing at a time	"I move to divide the question."

Motion	Second Required	Debatable	Amendable	Vote Required	Reconsider	Interrupt Speaker	Purpose	Form
Consideration Seriatim	yes	no	no	majority	no	no	To perfect each paragraph before voting	"I move to consider the question seriatim."
Division of the Group	no	no	no	none	no	yes	To verify an announced vote	"I call for a division of the Group."
Relating to Nominations	yes	no	no	$\frac{2}{3}$	no	no	To prevent additional nominations	"I move that nominations be closed."
Parliamentary Inquiry and Point of Information	no	no	no	none	no	yes	To provide parliamentary and other information	"I rise to a parliamentary inquiry."
Withdraw or Modify a Motion	no	no	no	none	no	no	To withdraw motion before it is voted on	"I request permission to withdraw my motion."

Unclassified or Miscellaneous Motions

Motion	Second Required	Debatable	Amendable	Vote Required	Reconsider	Interrupt Speaker	Purpose	Form
Take from Table¹	yes	no	no	majority	no	no	To bring up a motion previously tabled	"I move the motion be taken from the table."
Reconsider	yes	yes	no	majority	no	yes	To try to secure a new vote	"I move to reconsider...."
Rescind*	yes	yes	yes	majority with notice; or ⅔	negative only	no	To void or repeal action of the past	"I move that we rescind the motion previously passed."
Ratify*	yes	yes	yes	majority	yes	no	To make valid action already taken	"I move that...."

Incidental Motions have equal rank. Other incidentals may arise during a meeting.
Unclassified Motions are out of order if made when another motion is pending.
¹Must be made during the meeting or at the next meeting.   *Also may be a main motion.

CHAPTER **8**

SPECIAL EVENTS FOR AN ORGANIZATION

SPECIAL EVENTS in the life of any organization keep the group vital and strong. These highlights are significant for creating good memories and breaking the monotony of the regular business meeting.

INSTALLATION AND INITIATION CEREMONIES

Formal installation ceremonies for new officers can be very simple or very elaborate, depending on the wishes of the group. Sometimes the retiring president simply hands the gavel over to the incoming president, either at a regular meeting or at a joint meeting of the old and new Executive Boards. This transaction takes place with the introduction of New Business, and the incoming president presides after that. Other groups may have a social event, such as a luncheon, at which the retiring president is presented with a gift and in turn, hands over a presidential pin to a successor along with the gavel.

Most associations like to have some sort of formal installation ceremony as a special way to inaugurate the new officers because it gives importance to their function, provides a sense of order and continuity, and has the psychological value of allowing the officers to affirm solemnly that they will perform their roles to the best of their abilities.

Here is a very brief installation ritual whereby the president and other elected officers are sworn in by an installer, who can be a former officer of the association, or even a revered club member.

Installer: "Do you agree to discharge the duties of your respective offices faithfully and to the best of your ability?"

Officers: "I do."

Installer: "I now declare these officers duly installed."

A slightly longer service could run something like this.

Installer: "(Name of club) has been established to (recite club objectives). In order to achieve these high goals we must have officers who will perform diligently the duties assigned them. We are now gathered to install new officers of this club and to pledge anew our individual allegiances to its high calling."

"(Name of president), you have been chosen to lead this group, which will be measured by the manner in which you conduct its affairs. Tact, humor, sincerity, patience, self-control, open-mindedness, humility, fairness, and ability to work hard are attributes you should strive to possess. You must delegate responsibility without losing authority and conduct meetings impartially according to well-established rules. Do you promise to the best of your ability to assume and discharge the obligations of this office?"

President: "I do."

Installer: "(Name of vice president), you too have been given a responsible position. In the absence of the president you will preside over meetings and assume the office of president if it becomes vacant. Yours is the task of devising programs for the edification and delight of the membership. Do you promise to assist the president wholeheartedly and to carry out your assignments with enthusiasm?"

Vice president: "I do."

Installer: "(Name of secretary), yours is one of the most important positions in this organization, for you are the keeper of our records, which define our past and guide our future actions. You will record the transactions at the meetings, preserving the minutes with care and attention to detail. You will deal with all matters of correspondence in a manner to enlighten the group and to reflect credit on the society with others. Do you promise to fulfill all your obligations and to cooperate fully with the other officers?"

Secretary: "I do."

Installer: "(Name of treasurer), your office demands meticulous attention to detail and scrupulous care in handling the club's money. Do you promise to be honest, accurate, and efficient in receiving and disbursing club funds and to make full accounting of them to the membership?"

Treasurer: "I do."

Installer: "I now declare these offices of the (name of club) duly installed." (Speaking to members) "Do you as members promise to uphold the ideals of the club, to cooperate with these officers to the fullest, and to work diligently to carry to successful accomplishment the endeavors of the organization this year?"

Members: "We do."

Installer: "May the next term of office be memorable in the annals _____ Club."

Large national organizations such as the PTA and the National Honor Society have suggested installation programs which local chapters can use or adapt as they see fit. One popular style of installation involves a candlelight ceremony, with each candle standing for some aspect of the society's purpose or function, or symbolizing some quality of leadership inherent in each office. Often someone with writing talent can be delegated to prepare a ceremony which can become an anticipated tradition each year. The one common denominator of all such ceremonies is that the officers promise, singly or in unison, to be diligent in carrying out their responsibilities.

Similarly, new members may be initiated. An initiation ritual is especially appropriate for societies that "tap" members because of excellence according to some established criteria. For instance, in high schools, members of the local chapter of the National Honor Society must have a high grade average and excel in leadership, character, and service. To be asked to join the society is indeed a high honor, so the initiation ceremony usually is a high point of the spring semester, with parents attending, a special invited speaker, and recognition being given before the entire student body to serve as an incentive for others to strive to achieve.

Some groups escort candidates for membership onto a stage where club officers make brief remarks about the nature and purpose of the society, possibly lighting symbolic candles. Then the initiates receive a membership pin or card, are greeted ceremonially, and a social hour follows.

In any event, when newcomers join a group, they should be formally recognized by the chair, and all members should give them a warm welcome.

FUND RAISING

Another event common to practically all clubs is fund-raising. While the paying of dues by individual members helps defray part of the cost of an organization, the time will come, with rare exceptions, when additional money is needed.

Almost everyone is familiar with some of the events that are commonly held to raise funds: cookie sales, spaghetti suppers, door-to-door vending for band trips, raffles, and garage sales.

What must be borne in mind, however, is the fact that in each of these and other such events someone must be in charge. There must be careful planning and scheduling plus a lot of hard work if the fund-raiser is to be a success.

Another necessary ingredient is enthusiasm—something that is not hard to instill if the planning group is a high school band and the event a trip to march at the presidential inauguration or in the Orange Bowl parade. However, the situation is different if the organization is made up of middle-aged members of a church and the goal is to raise funds to buy handbells. In the latter instance, there will nevertheless be a few members who are highly motivated—as, for instance, those who visualize themselves as becoming a part of the handbell choir.

There will, of course, be variations, but generally there are certain rules that must be followed for any fund-raiser.

The first step is to decide what project would be the most suitable. It is important to consider the interests of the membership, the amount of money needed, and the kind of activity that is most suited to the talents and energies of the members.

Young people, for instance, have the interests and energy to make a car wash a success. Senior citizens might be more likely to participate in a sale of rare books or coins.

A popular kind of event nowadays is the garage sale, and it can be as large or as small as the resources of the members will allow. It can be a yard sale, assuming there is an alternative place in case of rain, or it can be at a school auditorium, a gymnasium, a church, or some other centrally located place.

It is absolutely essential that a chair and a co-chair be named, and they must be chosen with great care. The chair must have the ability and the desire to make the project succeed. She must be able to work with others, to delegate responsibility and perhaps most important of all, to inspire enthusiasm and a willingness to work.

The chair must do detailed planning, such as selecting a place for the event to be held and a date. Other details include the setting of a budget, estimating expenses, and calculating profits to be realized.

The co-chair must work closely with the chair and be prepared to take over if for any reason the chair cannot complete his duties.

There should also be a committee to work with the two leaders so that all functions of the event can be carried out in the most efficient manner possible.

Publicity is an important part of the successful fund-raiser. The organization can consider itself fortunate if it has a trained public relations specialist to take care of this function.

Since most fund-raisers are not particularly newsworthy, a special kind of publicity is needed. Making flyers, using billboards, and certainly using the organization's newsletter are ways to alert the membership and the public to the time, place, and other details of the event.

Attention to certain financial aspects is vital. It is most helpful if it can be announced that purchases of various items are tax deductible, which can be determined by checking with the Internal Revenue Service or someone else who is trained in such matters.

It is important that accurate records be kept of expenses and collections. These are matters for the treasurer to attend to, and a full reporting should be made to the membership of expenses, collections, and profits.

Financial records should be submitted in the form of a report to the president and a copy should be retained for future use, should it be decided to repeat the event or conduct something similar in the future.

FORUMS, PANEL DISCUSSIONS, DEBATES, SYMPOSIA

There are special types of programs that are common to most organizations. Among these are forums, panel discussions, debates, and symposia.

A *forum* usually is a lecture by one or more persons, with people from the audience then allowed to ask questions. If the subject is one that is generally familiar to most in the audience, the speeches can be dispensed with and those in the audience can ask questions or make comments to the "experts," who presumably can give intelligent answers.

Forums often involve highly controversial subjects and the person in charge of one must possess a rare combination of tact, patience, and wisdom to assure that the event runs smoothly.

Panel discussions appear on the surface to be simple events requiring no special direction, but this is far from the truth. Although there is normally a panel of "experts" ready and able to do their part, the chair is responsible for presenting the subject in such a way that the main points are brought out. She must then guide the discussion in such a way that audience participation will be encouraged.

The challenge for an organization that must choose persons for a panel discussion is to find those who are to appear, bearing in mind that "experts" often require an honorarium. The president or chair who is responsible should find out what fees must be paid and make sure that any agreements are made within the budget limitations of the organization.

At the close of a panel discussion, the chair should summarize the main points made by the panelists, being careful not to show bias toward either side.

Most Americans are familiar with the classic form of *debate* in which one or more persons presents the "pro" of an issue and one or more gives the "con" side. For the average organization, a debate usually consists of two persons, often public figures, debating the two sides of some controversial issue. If the debate is to be politically oriented, the services of the two participants can often be obtained free, especially if the debaters hold or aspire to public office.

Before an organization decides to hold a debate, it must have an interest in some particular subject. For instance, the League of Women Voters might be inspired to conduct a debate in which two sides of a tax issue can be discussed. The person in charge would contact the principals and make arrangements for the event to be held.

Such decisions as to the time and place must be made, along with the expenses that might be incurred.

A debate of this kind has great public interest, so the services of the organization's public relations representative would be needed.

The person in charge of the debate must meet with the principals and agreement made as to the ground rules—the length of time each will speak, the amount of rebuttal time, and limitations on the subject to be debated, for instance.

The debate chairman must adhere strictly to the guidelines that have been agreed upon and must be totally fair and impartial throughout, regardless of the private feelings of that person or the organization. The chairman must also see that the debaters receive courteous treatment from the audience and that good manners prevail, whatever the feelings of the audience.

A *symposium* is yet another type of program involving speakers and audiences. It is usually limited to a single subject, although it can be a broad one—the works of Southern writers, for instance.

Usually several speakers are invited, all of them knowledgeable about their subjects, although not necessarily in agreement on their points of view. A person arranging a symposium should set up the program in such a way that the most popular speaker will be scheduled at a time when the attendance will be the largest. After the speakers have made their presentations—or during them if this is agreeable to all concerned—the audience is encouraged to participate.

In preparing for a symposium, it is vital that the person in charge of public relations publicize the event. Symposia rarely have a captive audience, as it were, so the persons who can be expected to attend must be informed well ahead of time as to who the guests will be, the subject to be discussed, where it will take place, and the date, time and the cost, if any.

An organization's membership can be notified through the newsletter and by announcements at meetings. If the public is to be part of the audience, use must be made of such media outlets as newspapers, radio, and television.

CONVENTIONS

For the large organization it can be said that the convention is one of the major events of the entire year, and the planning for one begins during the convention preceding.

At a typical convention, new officers are elected and the committees are appointed whose specific purpose is to plan and be responsible for the convention for the following year. Probably the most important of these is the *Program Committee.* It should be authorized to arrange for speakers, set the dates and times that various subjects are to be discussed, and take care of numerous other details.

It is a good idea for the committee to be given authority to perform these functions through the bylaws. One of the first orders of business of a convention should be the adoption of the committee's program.

It is the responsibility of the president to appoint the Program Committee, and it should be done several months before the date of the convention.

The committee must work up its program well in advance of the convention date so that it can be given maximum publicity. If the organization has a newsletter or other type of publication circulated among the members, the program should be printed in it. Programs are also an important way of getting publicity, for a person can tell from a quick glance at a program if newsworthy people or events are included.

Copies of the program must, of course, be provided for all members and others who attend the convention. The Program Committee serves until the end of the convention, so that it can take care of any last minute details.

It is the duty of the *Credentials Committee* to see that only those persons with the proper credentials be allowed to take part in the business of the convention.

Delegates and alternates to a convention are furnished with certificates, commonly known as credentials. These should be signed by the secretary, and some organizations require that they also contain the president's signature.

Since conventions often attract nonmembers as well as members, it is imperative that a quick and easy means be established for identifying bona fide members. Identification is best made by the preparation of badges for both members and those nonmembers who have been invited.

Voting on various issues is, or course, limited to members and it is up to the Credentials Committee to ensure that only members are voting. Often nonmembers will be excluded from sessions where voting takes place. In any event, Credentials Committee members must devise a simple way of distinguishing members from nonmembers, perhaps by issuing different types of badges to the members or presenting a card to each voter.

The organization's bylaws should stipulate the method and time of appointment of members of the Credentials Committee. This should be done by the president and well in advance of the convention so that the committee can be ready to examine credentials of delegates as they arrive.

Before any business is transacted, the Credentials Committee must report the number of delegates who are in attendance. A motion should be made to adopt the committee's report. The committee continues through the convention, making daily reports if additional delegates arrive.

No major event can be carried out without rules, and conventions are no exceptions. The bylaws of every organization should provide for the naming of a *Rules Committee*. Appointments are customarily made by the president and should be made early so that necessary rules will be established when the convention begins.

Here is a sample of what the rules might cover:

•Members should be in their seats five minutes before the scheduled starting time for the various meetings.

•All resolutions must be referred to the Resolutions Committee.

•Nominating speeches shall be limited to three minutes.

•Any delegate may rise to speak, provided he obtains recognition from the presiding officer.

•Debate shall be limited to five minutes for each speaker.

•Debate on any question shall be limited to a total of twenty minutes.

It is furthermore the duty of the Rules Committee to see that its rules are enforced, and it should at all times have the full support of the president and other ranking officers of the organization.

It is the function of the *Resolutions Committee* to conduct meetings and consider various proposals for submission to the full membership for a vote. These proposals should be written in the form of resolutions. Here is an abbreviated sample:

"Whereas increasing enrollment at Smith County High School has overtaxed existing facilities, and

Whereas efforts to increase the property tax have met with failure, and

Whereas the quality of education has suffered, due to the large number of pupils that must be assigned each teacher,

Now therefore be it resolved that the Smith County High School PTA go on record as urging the calling of a referendum to provide for an increase in the local sales tax of one cent on each dollar.

Resolutions are acted upon by a meeting of the full membership usually near the end of the convention. Their adoption or rejection is done through a vote of the membership, usually a majority of those present and voting. They are formally presented one at a time by the chair.

The president should appoint the Resolutions Committee several months before the date of the convention so that a number of meetings can be held to consider various proposals of interest to the organization.

The adoption of resolutions is often a source of news—for instance, a resolution such as the sample just given represents an organization's collective view on whether another tax should be added, and this is always news. Thus the public relations representative should see to it that the media is informed of the action that has been taken.

It is the responsibility of the *Nominating Committee* to see to it that the best officers possible be chosen to continue the work of the organization. Often members of the committee are elected at the previous year's convention.

A Nominating Committee usually meets well before a convention and makes its selections. The committee should be composed of people who are knowledgeable about the membership and whose only concern is to see that the best possible people are chosen for the responsibilities that will be assigned them.

Before nominating a person for a post, that person should be contacted to make certain that she is willing to serve. Some organizations add spice to the selection of officers by providing for the nomination of two persons to be voted on for each office.

The method of electing officers varies considerably, depending on the size of the organization. Often competition is keen among persons vying for an office. In other cases, it is difficult to find people who are willing to serve.

If the election of officers is held in a large convention it is a good idea to have a number of stationary ballot boxes located in the area where the voting is taking place. Tellers should be posted to take up the ballots, which should be either folded or given to them face down. Only one printed ballot is given to each delegate. If a person spoils the ballot, it must be returned so that another can be obtained.

If the organization is a small one, considerably less formality is needed. It is up to each club to decide on the method best suited to its needs, bearing in mind the need for fairness and courtesy to those who are vying for the office.

If a person is elected to more than one office, the candidate may choose the one he prefers. If the candidate is absent, the club should decide which office to fill by a majority voice vote. If two candidates receive a tie vote, the assembly should continue balloting, or the two may decide by lot.

It is obvious from the foregoing that the success or failure of a convention is largely up to the committees that run it. It is also obvious that no effort should be spared in seeing that care be taken in the selection of those who will direct and serve on the committees of the organization.

PUBLIC RELATIONS

No matter what the organization, good public relations is a must. It can help make special events such as fund-raising a success, draw contributions into the treasury, increase membership, contribute to success of various endeavors, and give the society's members pride in their group.

Many definitions of public relations have been made, one of which is, "Public relations consists of doing the right thing and letting the world know about it." Whatever the definition, there is no question but that everyone wants to put the best foot forward and let people know about the good things being done.

A valuable member of each managerial team is the person whose responsibility it is to handle public relations. If it is a small group, the PR person can handle that function along with whatever other duties may be required.

Basically, there are two major types of public relations—internal and external.

Internal public relations is directed toward people within an organization. The person who is the official PR representative should impress upon the other members that good PR is everybody's job and should be practiced both inside and outside the group.

When the club holds a meeting, members, particularly the newly initiated, should be made to feel welcome by officers and others of longer standing. The key word is friendliness, and when there are guests they also should receive a cordial greeting.

It is the responsibility of the public relations chair to see that members are kept informed of what is going on in the organization. One way to accomplish this is through a newsletter. In writing a newsletter, brevity is the key to a widely read document. Often the information can all be put on a single sheet, or at least on the front and back of a sheet.

Content is the main ingredient, so it is not necessary to produce a fancy product. A newsletter should contain such information as a message from the president, announcement of details of the next meeting, special activities of the group, and interesting facts about members. If a member receives a special honor outside the organization, that should certainly be reported as should other personal happenings—someone's birthday, the arrival of a new baby or grandchild, an impending marriage, an unusual vacation. So it is important to have a network of news sources in addition to receiving official news from the president and Executive Board.

In addition to serving the members, a newsletter can become a good form of external public relations when copies are sent to interested persons outside the organization. For instance, a religion editor of a newspaper reports that the best source of news about church activities within the city comes from the newsletter mailed to her from the various churches.

External public relations begins at home, with every member responsible for letting people know about the organization's attributes. Word of mouth is a splendid means of attracting new members.

One of the most valuable tools for informing people about an organization is through the preparation of a brochure. While everyone would like to produce a fancy, four-color brochure (and this is fine if a group can afford it), there are less expensive ways to produce one. If the organization is a low-budget one, it might prove helpful to check out a small print shop for the printing and reproduction work. Often a member of the organization has facilities for reproduction, especially for photocopying.

In preparing a brochure, it must be borne in mind that something more than the bare facts is needed. A brochure must do a selling job; it must make a pleasing impression on the reader. The writing should reflect an enthusiastic attitude, without overdoing it, and there should be pictures to support what is written—pictures of the officers, perhaps a scene at the last convention, a typical meeting or outing, a shot of a group working at a fund-raising event. If the organization has a logo, it should be used on the brochure, letterheads, and other materials.

Good brochures sell not only outsiders but the members of an organization as well. Ways should be found to get them in the hands of people who may be of help to the organization, and that includes prospective members. Therefore they should be sure to include pertinent facts about the organization, its history, goals, purposes, and activities. As in any good writing, the style should be clear and concise with the writer ever mindful of the fact that most people do not spend a lot of time reading brochures.

The media are such an important part of public relations that many people get the impression that they are the only kind of public relations. In any event, the importance of good media contacts cannot be over-emphasized, and there are a few simple rules that should be followed in all dealings with the media.

The essence of media relations is the recognition of the fact that an organization has something to tell that would appeal either to the public in general or to a significant part of it. It is helpful to have someone in charge of this function who has a background in news or is at least knowledgeable about it.

Newsworthy events in the life of an organization that make news include the election of officers, the holding of conventions, fund-raising events open to the public, meetings in which some topic of public interest is dealt with, and accomplishments of individual members. If a prominent official is to be a guest speaker, it is often newsworthy, particularly if the official plans to discuss a subject of widespread interest.

Occasionally the public relations person may have to write a news release that tells about an upcoming event. It should be typed, double-spaced, and brief, while giving all essential details. There is nothing wrong with preparing a simple fact sheet, provided it contains all the necessary facts.

If the public relations person can spare the time, it is better to take the news release or fact sheet to the newspaper, radio, or television station and hand it to the person who most likely might be interested in it. One advantage of having media contacts is that the PR person can inquire easily as to which person or department might be interested in the news being announced.

Newspapers nowadays have many specialized sections, including suburban zones where happenings in a small nearby town or city get more elaborate treatment than if they were happening in a city. Also, do not underrate the small "throwaways" which are distributed free with news directed to small areas; they are widely read.

Often an event will be deemed worthy of a picture, and it is to the advantage of the PR person if the newspaper contact can be prevailed upon to send a photographer to take the picture. This will increase the odds tremendously that the event will receive coverage in the newspaper.

The electronic media offer various possibilities for exposure. Radio stations often invite organizations to send them notices of their meetings and other activities. Television stations are necessarily limited to more dramatic types of news, but if a PR person has something that might fill the bill, it certainly does not cost anything to call the assignments editor and find out.

With newspapers and television stations, remember that if there is a news story about a person or persons, then there is a very good possibility a picture of them can be used. A good, clean black and white head shot is best for a newspaper, preferably one that has been professionally taken. Television stations prefer color slides.

Not only in public relations but in all facets of an organization's life—laying the foundation, structuring the framework, setting up the internal functions, attending to business matters, conducting meetings, and running special events—it is necessary to plan thoroughly, to think creatively, to organize efficiently, and to arrange for periodic assessment of results. In addition, good common sense, courtesy, a willingness to cooperate and to work diligently are needed. A basic tool, such as this simple handbook, should be studied thoughtfully by officers, committee chairs, and members. The result then should be a viable organization that accomplishes its goals and makes a difference in its world.

PART TWO:

BASIC
PUBLIC
SPEAKING

CHAPTER 9

MEETING YOUR SPEAKING NEEDS

THIS SECTION of *The Basic Meeting Manual* is intended to be helpful to those who are called upon to speak in public and who want to become more confident in speaking and more effective in what they say. It is designed to offer practical guidelines to those who are willing to *prepare* and *practice* before they present any material in public.

The fact that you have made the effort to find this manual and are investing valuable time in reading it indicates that you want to do not just an adequate job with your speaking assignment, but a superior one. You are willing to devote the time and effort that it takes to excel.

You realize that you have a responsibility to your audience. Of course, you want to do well, but those who hear you also want you to do well. They want to be informed and inspired. They want you to use their time wisely, to contribute something to them. But to make a contribution—to move people—you must speak forcefully and convincingly.

This section will guide you to your full potential in communicating with people by providing general information for effective public speaking. By following the suggestions presented here, you will ultimately be able to speak clearly, fluently, and persuasively in any situation requiring you to speak in public. You will, in fact, reach the goal most desired by any public speaker—the ability to make a difference.

Perhaps you have accepted an office in a school or civic organization that requires you to communicate effectively with a group of people, or perhaps your business or church activities make it necessary for you to speak in public. You rightly feel that you need to speak as effectively as you can, because how well you speak will determine how much you are able to accomplish.

Never before has the ability to speak well been so important. The rapid growth in the twentieth century of the telephone, radio, and television industries attests to the fact that the spoken word is powerful. We listen, and we are persuaded by those who can express their ideas effectively. Those who can speak most convincingly become our political leaders, our executives, and our spiritual advisors.

There will be many times when you will need to communicate effectively. You may be asked to present a formal speech, but there will be many less formal occasions when you will need to be persuasive. You may want to engage in informal discussions, make comments at a PTA meeting, teach a Sunday school lesson, lead a public prayer, give demonstrations to a civic group, conduct an interview, respond to complaints, take part in panel discussions, conduct a meeting, talk with salespeople and reporters, or just explain something to family or friends.

In many of these situations, formal and informal, you will be *selling*—selling your ideas, your point of view. You are either for or against someone or something, and you are trying to persuade others to agree with you. You may be speaking one to one or one to many, but you are selling just the same.[1] You are persuading people.

According to Stephen E. Lucas, author of a widely accepted college textbook on public speaking, persuading people to do something you feel is right, informing people about what they did not already know, entertaining people and making them feel happy and good about themselves are the major goals of public speaking. It is through these opportunities that we have the chance "to make a difference, to change the world in some small way, to leave a mark of ourselves."[2]

We have discussed the importance of persuading people. Now let's consider the importance of effectively informing people about topics they are not familiar with. You should be able to communicate information in such a way that it can be clearly understood. The ancient Greek statesman Pericles said, "One who forms a judgment on any point but cannot explain himself clearly...might as well never have thought at all on the subject."[3] This is as true today as it was almost twenty-five centuries ago.

Informing people is simply sharing knowledge with them for their benefit. Your role, then, is to organize the information you possess and pass it to your hearers in a way that will cause them to understand what you have told them. If you make the effort to learn how to inform people skillfully, you will make a contribution in your sphere of influence.

In addition to persuading people and informing them, there is that third goal of public speaking—entertaining people. There are many ways to entertain people. You can amuse or inspire them; you can stimulate their intellects or emotions. If the content of your speech is interesting, and if it is well delivered, then it will entertain your audience. What's more, you will be a success.

Success in public speaking is what it's all about anyway. You may well feel uncertain about your ability to handle your task. Take heart in the fact that public speaking is a learned art; it is not something you are born with. It is an art that you acquire through experience and that you will continue to improve throughout your lifetime. Remember that it is an art that no one completely masters. You will be striving, then, not for perfection, but for improvement.

There are some simple guidelines that you can master which will increase your effectiveness in speaking. These are the same principles that have been used by great speakers down through the centuries, from Pericles to Ronald Reagan, and they will work for you also.

Speaking well, like writing well, requires a lot of hard work. It certainly has its price tag in the form of effort and time expended, but there is no doubt that the result is worth a lot more than it costs.

This first chapter has identified your speaking needs. The next chapter will identify that insidious enemy—stage fright. This enemy seems formidable, but it is easily destroyed if you use the right weapons. Chapter 10 will supply you with the weapons you need to put your adversary to flight and to speak with confidence.

CHAPTER **10**

GAINING CONFIDENCE

THE FIRST weapon that you need in your war against stage fright is an understanding of it. It is a well-known fact that we tend to fear what we do not understand. You need to understand the nature of this problem before you can take measures to control it.

You probably think that stage fright is a negative emotion. You may feel inadequate because you become nervous before speaking in public. You may even feel that there is something drastically wrong with you because you experience an irrational fear in a situation that you know holds no real danger. You may believe that since many appear to show no uneasiness at all when they rise to speak, that they must, then, be endowed with some innate quality that allows them to speak easily with no apparent agitation—a quality that you simply do not possess.

It should comfort you to know that you certainly are not the only one who suffers from stage fright. All beginners have stage fright. In fact, most experienced speakers and actors experience it—sometimes even after a thousand or more performances! Even Cicero, the greatest orator of ancient Rome, had stage fright. Twenty centuries ago he confessed, "I turn pale at the outset of a speech, and quake in every limb."[1]

Down through the ages successful athletes, politicians, actors, and other public figures have experienced it. You can be reassured by knowing that if you suffer from stage fright, you are in good company. What's more, unless you can find a cure that has eluded the experts for centuries, you will never fully recover from it—nor should you want to.

The "greats" in sports, politics, and theater do not regard stage fright as a negative force. Instead, they welcome the "butterflies in the stomach," the constricted throat, and the pounding heart as a positive force—one that can improve their performances. They insist that they rarely give an outstanding performance unless they first suffer the symptoms of stage fright. If they feel relaxed and comfortable, they almost always lack the "edge" they need to reach their maximum potential. They simply are not "psyched up." They have learned to use their nervousness to their advantage.

In order to understand stage fright, let's examine what causes this disturbing condition in the first place. Those who have made a scientific study of the phenomenon of stage fright tell us that it is the product of fear—fear of being mocked, fear of forgetting, fear of being unable to speak skillfully, fear of not measuring up to the expectations of the audience, fear of appearing ridiculous—in short, fear of being in some way inadequate in the situation.

Co-authors Virgil L. Baker, of the University of Arkansas, and Ralph T. Eubanks, of the University of West Virginia, suggest that the fear people experience in the form of stage fright is basically the same as that felt in any other challenging situation. The discus thrower waiting his turn at a field meet, a speeding driver hearing a police siren, and an army sergeant unexpectedly being summoned to company headquarters—all suffer the same internal and external manifestations of fear that the public speaker feels.[2]

By now you already possess one of the weapons needed to

combat this fear—the weapon of *understanding*. You understand that stage fright is universal, that it results from the fear of being inadequate, and that it can be sublimated to work as a positive force. Now let's consider another weapon—the weapon of *conviction*. The conviction that it is important to gain control over your anxiety is a major step toward effective speaking.

Speaking in public can be unsettling and anxiety-producing. Furthermore, the anxiety is not something that you can will away. It creeps upon you despite your firm resolve that it will not happen. Even if the tension may be helpful, it is certainly not pleasant.

Why, then, should you subject yourself to this kind of stress? Why willingly put yourself in a situation that you know will trigger such an irrational response? The answer is rooted in your birthright as an American. To deny yourself the ability to communicate as effectively as possible would be to deny your American heritage. It would be, in effect, to deny yourself the inalienable right of freedom of speech guaranteed to you in our Constitution.

Of what benefit to you is freedom of speech if you don't have the courage to use it? How can you make a difference without being heard? Why let others who have less to contribute than you make the wrong decisions without your even voicing an objection? Don't be one of the silent majority!

How many times have you sat in a meeting and had something you wanted to say, ideas you wanted to advance? But you lacked the courage to express them and simply sat there in silence, a victim of stage fright. Just because you haven't had the confidence to speak in public certainly does not mean that you have nothing to say. Your ideas are valuable.

Arm yourself with acceptance—accept the fact that you will always suffer some degree of stage fright when speaking in public. Kenneth McFarland states that it isn't necessary to banish fear completely in order to gain confidence. He believes that "a wholesome fear of failure is one of the best guarantees of success."[3]

Accept the fact that the apprehension you feel is not cowardly but natural. It is your response to it that makes the difference, making you either a coward or a hero. Accept every opportunity that comes your way to speak in public. The more you speak, the more relaxed you will be when speaking. Gaining experience is so important that you should even *make* opportunities to speak. You can be absolutely certain that if you force yourself to accept speaking assignments and to speak out at meetings, you will become more confident each time you do it. What's more, the confidence you acquire is progressive. According to Lucas, "it nurtures itself." He promises, "After you score your first triumph, you will be that much more confident the next time...." He also promises that the fears of speaking in public "will gradually recede until they are replaced by only a healthy nervousness...."[4]

If you have the courage to gain experience—to meet the enemy head on, time after time—if you make yourself appear in public, you will gain a little with every encounter and will be able to keep your enemy at bay.

You are now armed with an understanding of stage fright, with a conviction that you need to master it, and with an acceptance of the fact that it is ever present. But there is yet another weapon you will need, which is actually the most important one of all—careful, painstaking *preparation.* So important is thorough preparation to your success that we will devote the next six chapters to helping you make that adequate preparation which is so necessary for confident speaking.

CHAPTER **11**

ANALYZING YOUR SPEAKING SITUATION

SINCE YOU know that stage fright is the result of the fear of being inadequate, you must now take the steps that will control this fear and build your confidence. Confidence defeats stage fright, and the better prepared you are to give your speech, the more confident you will be.

You must be prepared to spend a lot of time doing your homework. You can expect to spend much more time in preparing a speech than in presenting one. But how do you know where to begin your preparation?

There are certain general guidelines to follow. First of all, you should consider the occasion for which you will be speaking. If you are to deliver a formal, thirty-minute speech before a large group, obviously your preparation will be different from your preparation for presenting a plan to a small committee. Each occasion, of course, requires careful preparation, since it is just as important to be effective in presenting a brief proposal as in presenting a lengthy, formal speech. In each case you will be trying to make a difference. But your preparation should be consistent with your task.

Since every speech occasion is different, you will have to

prepare differently for each one. You should know the purpose of the meeting and the size of the expected audience. You should know the time, the place, and the mood of the gathering. You should also know what else will be included in the program and how much time will be given for your presentation. Then you should know whether your presentation should be formal or informal, informative or merely entertaining, detailed or general, brief or lengthy. In short, you should be able to adjust your presentation to fit the circumstances.

After considering the occasion on which you will be speaking, you should next give careful attention to your audience. They are entrusting you with one of their most valuable and usually least plentiful assets—their time. You are obligated to fill it wisely. They earnestly hope that you will inform, instruct, inspire, or entertain them. To waste their time through your lack of understanding of their needs and backgrounds or through your lack of adequate preparation would be to violate their trust.

You must first carefully analyze your audience, then adapt your ideas to them and to the particular occasion. You should consider such factors as age, sex, education, economic level, religion, cultural and ethnic backgrounds. Most audiences have a wide range of knowledge, interests, ideas, values, opinions, and behaviors. By analyzing all of these elements and adjusting your presentation to the concerns and background of your audience, you will be able to construct for them a speech that will spark and hold their interest.

Also, you must be careful to talk in terms your audience can understand, not at a level above their knowledge and experience. Otherwise, they may receive a message totally different from the one you intended.

Obviously, then, it is imperative that you determine what

the members of your particular audience "know and believe"—that you analyze that audience before preparing to speak before them. Your task may be difficult if your audience is composed of men and women from different age groups or from different economic and cultural levels. Of course, you cannot adapt to each individual in your audience, but you can try to make your comments meaningful to the majority. The skill with which you do this will determine to a great extent how effective you will be as their speaker.

The following considerations are of major importance in audience analysis:

Age

A person's age substantially affects his outlook. Members of each generation have certain experiences and values that are common to them and that are not shared by previous or succeeding generations. If you have an audience composed of members of several generations, you will need to explain references to events that are beyond the lifetime of the younger members. Also, keep in mind that the values of the older members may differ from your own or from those of younger members.

Sex

As a modern speaker you need to consider that the rigid sex roles of the past are disappearing. The thinking of men and women has changed in regard to what is appropriate for each. We find men and women working on an equal basis in such areas as business, medicine, education, government, the military, and even in domestic duties and professional sports. There are certain distinctions, particularly on a social level, that need to be considered. You can still expect that an audience composed of men only will have a greater understanding of football and car engines and that an audience of women only will have a greater understanding of cooking and sewing, even though the exact opposite may be true in certain individual instances. The main consideration is that you avoid thinking in terms of outmoded stereotypes but instead recognize any valid distinctions that do still exist.

Religion

If you bring into your speech any material of a religious nature, you need to consider the fact that your audience may in no way share your religious views. You may be addressing people whose religious beliefs vary widely, not only from yours, but from each other's. Your audience may include atheists, agnostics, Roman Catholics, Jews, Mormons, Baptists, Presbyterians, evangelical Christians, Buddhists, and Muslims. You do not have to surrender, or even compromise, your own personal beliefs in dealing with material that is religiously oriented. But you do need to find ways to be tactful and to show common courtesy and good manners in your treatment of such material. Failure to do so can weaken or even destroy your effectiveness.

Cultural Background

If you are addressing a general audience, you can expect wide differences in the cultural backgrounds represented by this group. There may be people from other countries present, but even among citizens of the United States you will find people whose foreign descent will cause them to hold widely differing customs and beliefs. Be aware of these, especially if there will be a large number of any particular cultural group in the audience. A careless racial or ethnic slur may cause an inflammatory reaction from your audience, which will instantly destroy your credibility.

Knowledge

Taking into consideration the amount of knowledge that the audience has about your topic will be invaluable in preparing your speech. It will allow you to adjust what you say to what they already know. If they have little knowledge of your subject, you will need to present it on an elementary level; if they are more knowledgeable, of course, you can be more technical in your presentation. By starting where they are, and then by phrasing your message so that it is readily understood by them, you will have a much greater chance of succeeding as their speaker.

Size

In preparing for your presentation you need to take into account the size of your expected audience to determine how you treat your subject. If your audience is large, you will need to be more formal in your delivery, in your choice of words, in your illustrations, and in your use of visual aids. A smaller group lends itself to a more informal, intimate style and allows greater flexibility in the use of visual aids.

There are other important considerations for audience analysis. You will need to make every effort to get in tune with your audience by studying their interests, backgrounds, and attitudes. But you may wonder how to get such information about them.

A good way to learn about your audience is to talk with the person who has invited you to speak. That contact will usually be able to give you a good description of your audience and their expectations of you as their speaker. Talking with others who have spoken to the same group and getting their evaluation of audience response and attitudes may also be helpful. Knowing what clubs the members of your audience belong to may also help in your assessment. Do they belong to labor unions, the Chamber of Commerce, the American Medical Association, the National Organization for Women, the Young Republicans, the Crusade for Christ? Knowing their club affiliations will be revealing in trying to determine the attitudes and background of your listeners.

If your speaking occasion is formal, you can use interviews and questionnaires, even professional pollsters, to gain information about the background of that particular audience. In most cases, however, you will be able to obtain adequate information about your audience by using the simpler methods that have been mentioned. What is important is getting the feel of your audience so that you can relate to them in the best possible way.

You have seen in this chapter that the preliminary steps of analyzing your speaking occasion and your audience are of utmost importance. To get the rest of the way you simply need to apply what you have learned about your audience situation to the actual preparation of your speech. Chapter 12 will guide you through this step as you continue your preparation for filling your assignment.

CHAPTER 12

SELECTING YOUR TOPIC

ONCE YOU have obtained the necessary information about your speaking occasion and have carefully evaluated the background and needs of your audience, you can turn your attention to another important matter—your topic. Of course, many times your topic will be assigned to you, or the nature of your responsibilities will determine your choice of subject matter. But if you are simply asked to speak on a subject of your own choosing, you must select a suitable topic to fit the occasion and the audience.

In making your selection, first be sure that your subject matter is appropriate for the occasion. Most people don't want to hear political speeches in church or sermons in Congress, nor will they tolerate a flagrant misuse of the occasion. Any speaker who tries to exploit a speaking opportunity to advance a personal cause will almost certainly incur the wrath of the audience.

Second, be sure that your treatment of the subject is appropriate to its importance. A serious theme, for instance, should not be treated in a frivolous or flippant manner, but with dignity and reserve. Third, be sure that your topic is one they will believe you are qualified to discuss. They will consider your age, your grasp of the subject, and your experience. Ask yourself this question: "Does the topic conform reasonably well to the image your listeners have of your reputation, status, maturity, appearance?"[1] If it does, you are on the right track. Of course, being knowledgeable as a speaker is important, but expertise alone is not enough.

An audience's receptivity to a message is invariably affected by their perception of the speaker. Cato the Elder of ancient Rome observed, "An orator is a good man who is skilled in speaking." An audience must have confidence in a speaker's integrity. We tend to believe those whom we trust, and we are skeptical of those we distrust. It takes more objectivity than most audiences possess to separate the message from the messenger. Most often we must believe in the individual first before we can accept what the speaker is saying. You must establish your credibility as a speaker for your particular audience, for without credibility nothing you say can be of any significance.

Let's look now at another important consideration in selecting a suitable topic: the specific response you want from your audience. You need to decide whether your speaking occasion will require you to persuade, inform, or entertain your audience. Knowing your purpose will not only help you choose an appropriate topic, but it will also enable you to gather the most effective materials for accomplishing it. In addition it will help you choose the most appropriate style and language to use in your presentation.

As you continue your search for a suitable topic, there is another prime consideration: gaining the interest and attention of the audience. Lucas observes that "no matter how well you construct your speeches, they are likely to fall flat unless you speak about matters of interest to your listeners."[2] Choosing a topic that will command the attention of your audience, then, is of utmost importance.

And what interests people?

Very simply, they usually want to hear about things that are meaningful to them. People are *egocentric*. They pay closest attention to messages that affect their own values, their own beliefs, their own well-being. Listeners typically approach speeches with one question uppermost in mind: Why is this important to *me*?[3]

A subject is more likely to interest an audience:

- If it is of vital concern to them in their daily affairs
- If it is in the news, and therefore, timely
- If it offers a solution to a problem they are trying to solve
- If it is a subject that is controversial
- If it is a subject that they already know something about

Choosing such a subject will assure you, at least initially, of a certain amount of audience attention. Continuing to hold their attention, however, depends largely on the skill with which you provide additional background information and on your ability to speak on their level of knowledge.

Even though speaking on one of the topics just mentioned is a good way of gaining the attention of the audience, it is not the only way. It is certainly possible to gain their attention and hold it by introducing a subject that is entirely new to them. In fact, you can take any topic that you are interested in and make it interesting to almost any audience. If you choose as a topic one that matters to you, your interest will ignite the subject matter for your audience. You will be much more likely to have something worthwhile to say if you have a genuine interest in your subject.

There is one last consideration in the selection of a topic. Choose a subject that you can cover adequately in the time allotted to you. Perhaps the most important rule of etiquette in public speaking is that *you must finish on time.* Your topic should not be so technical that it would require too many time-consuming explanations nor should it be too wide in scope. It is far better to cover one aspect of a broader subject in an interesting, relaxed manner than to try to cram too much information into a hurried presentation. Try, then, to choose a topic that you can cover thoroughly and interestingly in whatever length of time you are privileged to have, whether it is five minutes or fifty minutes.

Thus, the selection of a suitable topic will always involve careful consideration, but it is certainly worth the time and effort it takes. After you are satisfied that you have selected a topic that is appropriate for your audience and meaningful to them, you must turn your attention to gathering the materials that will enable you to speak most convincingly on your subject. Chapter 13 provides important guidelines for you to use in doing the necessary research in preparing to speak.

CHAPTER **13**

PREPARING TO DO RESEARCH

IT IS your responsibility as a speaker to provide the most accurate information available in your subject area. To do this successfully may require a great deal of research on your part. White cites presidents Kennedy, Nixon, Ford, Carter, and Reagan as examples of effective speakers who have been diligent in making careful preparation for their speaking opportunities. Then he asks this question: "If established and successful speakers, almost without exception, recognize the importance of painstaking preparation, can you afford to slight research in your speech preparation?"[1] And, of course, the answer is no!

If you exercise the self-discipline that is required for doing careful research, your efforts will be rewarded with positive audience response. The speaker who makes the greatest impact is the one who is persistent in her preparation.

In order to research your subject efficiently, first you will need to equip yourself with a generous supply of index cards, preferably of the 4 x 6 or 5 x 8 size. Select the size you like best and then use only cards of that size, since that will make it easier for you to shuffle through them later and organize them. Index cards will enable you to record your material in the most efficient way possible.

GUIDELINES FOR USING INDEX CARDS

• Write only on the front side of each card. Then, when you actually begin composing your speech or presentation, you will be able to lay your cards out on a desk or table and see at a glance the material on each one.

• Use a separate card for every idea. Then, later on, as your ideas develop and as you arrive at certain general topics you want to cover, you can go back and at the top of each card, label it according to the *category* into which it falls. You can later sort out all the cards that pertain to each category and put them in separate piles. When you actually begin writing your speech, you will have before you, in organized form, all the material that you have gathered in each category.

• Make a separate bibliography card for each source you use. For books record the name of the author, title, place of publication, publisher and date of publication. For magazine articles record the name of the author (if given), title of the article, name of the magazine, date of publication, and page numbers. This detailed information is important in case someone should ask you for information about your source or in the event that you later want to publish your speech.

• Make a notation on each card of the source of the information on that card. At the top of the card—but leaving enough space to fill in the category later on—record the author's last name, the title of the book or article, and the page number. (You will already have the complete information on the bibliography card.) Then write down the material you wish to remember. Sometimes you will simply use your own words to rephrase an idea. If you plan to quote a certain passage verbatim, you should enclose the material in quotation marks and be certain that you have copied it accurately.

If you prepare index cards according to this method it will

not only give you a better grasp of your overall topic, but it will save time as well.

In researching a speech you should look for the following information categories:

- Facts
- Definitions
- Descriptions
- Opinions
- Observations
- Illustrations
- Comparisons
- Statistics
- Visual Aids

These are the elements from which you can construct a well-developed speech. Of course, you may not need to use every one of these information areas for your particular speaking assignment, but this list will provide some important guidelines. You should give special attention to four of the items in the list: illustrations, comparisons, statistics, and visual aids.

First, let's consider the importance of using good *illustrations* in your speech. An illustration is an easily remembered story that will help your audience understand the point you are trying to make.

Proodian advises, "Talk in stories and illustrations, not statements of principle. Make your words paint pictures of people and places. Transform numbers and percentages. For example, change 20 percent to one of every five of you." He believes that illustrations such as these are far better than generalizations and abstractions and that they will be much more meaningful to your audience.[2]

Illustrations may be either (a) *factual*—based on fact—or (b) *hypothetical*—made up to suit a purpose. Grasty and Newman provide us with the following examples to illustrate the difference between the two:

(a) There are people who have overcome such handicaps. For example, Franklin D. Roosevelt, though struck down with infantile paralysis....

(b) A person's health is an important factor in his usefulness to society. For example, suppose that tomorrow morning you should suddenly become seriously ill....[3]

The use of illustrations is one of the most time-honored methods of lending support to an idea or opinion. We find in the New Testament that Jesus used stories—commonly referred to as parables—almost exclusively in His teachings. Reading these allows you to observe the effective use of those illustrations which rank as the greatest of all time.

Lucas gives four helpful tips for using illustrations successfully:

1) Use real illustrations whenever possible.

2) Use illustrations that are representative—that do not deal with unusual or exceptional cases.

3) Use illustrations that relate directly to the point you are trying to make.

4) Make your illustrations vivid by supplying the everyday details that bring them to life and create a sense of reality.[4]

You can use these tips as guidelines while doing your research. They will help you while you look for effective illustrations that will enable you to make the greatest impact upon your audience.

The use of *comparisons* (analogies) is another effective way to help your audience grasp the ideas you are trying to communicate. Using analogies is a method by which the unknown is compared with the known, and similarities or differences are noted.

A comparison, as White notes, can be either *figurative*, comparing objects or ideas of different classes ("as a man to a mountain, a government to a ship, a countenance to a thundercloud or charity to rain")[5] or *literal*, comparing objects or ideas of the same class ("such as rivers to rivers, cities to cities").[6] Minnick presents the following examples to illustrate *figurative* and *literal* comparisons:

> If you said that a factory resembles a beehive in its organization and distribution of labor, you would be using a figurative analogy. If, on the other hand, you said that the Ford assembly plant in Marietta, Georgia operates like the Oldsmobile assembly plant in Lansing, Michigan, you would be using a literal analogy.[7]

The use of comparisons helps your audience comprehend ideas or figures that are outside of their range of experience and understanding. Hedde, Brigance and Powell give the following example: "If you say, 'Switzerland has less than one-sixth the area of Colorado' (or is less than three times the area of Connecticut), its size takes on greater meaning for your listeners."[8]

Lucas provides another similar example by suggesting that you could help an audience fathom the idea that stars are trillions of miles apart in this way: "To give you an idea how vast the distance between stars is, if there were just three bees in the whole United States, the air would be more congested with bees than space is with stars."[9] In doing your research, then, look for comparisons that will assist your audience in understanding the points you are trying to make.

Look also for appropriate *statistics*. The skillful use of statistics can often lend support to the ideas you are trying to emphasize.

There is no doubt that we are living in the age of calculators, word processors, and computers, and that the compilation of statistics is a relatively simple task because of advanced technology. It is also apparent that *we* are programmed to expect the use of statistics as supporting evidence and that many times we cannot be convinced without it. But this certainly does not mean that your speech should be composed mostly of statistics. Nothing can be more boring to an audience than a recitation of dry and uninteresting figures, and nothing will cause you to lose their attention more quickly.

The skillful use of statistics, on the other hand, can be a great asset to you in convincing your audience, if you are careful to follow certain guidelines.

SEVEN GUIDELINES GOVERNING THE USE OF STATISTICS

• *Use statistics sparingly.* Don't confuse your audience with a meaningless avalanche of facts and figures.

Use statistics only when they are needed to clarify a point, and then be sure you have made them easy to understand.

• *Use round numbers.* Unless there is a good reason for being more accurate, round off your figures. This makes them easier to understand and to remember. It is much easier to remember that Pikes Peak is 14,000 feet high than it is to try to remember that it is 14,110 feet high.

• *Be sure your statistics are valid.* Facts and figures can be distorted and made to prove almost anything. For this reason you should be sure that the statistics you are using have been gathered by reliable, objective, nonpartisan sources. In other words, you need to be certain that they are accepted by the experts, that they are verified by other findings, that they are representative, that they have been obtained from a large enough sampling, that they have been accurately reported and classified, and that they have been accurately interpreted. It is especially important to verify any statistics that you find in an ordinary newspaper or magazine article by referring to a recognized library reference book, such as the latest edition of the *World Almanac, Information Please*, the *Statistical Abstract of the United States, Statistical Yearbook*, or the *Guinness Book of World Records*.

• *Use other forms of support in conjunction with your statistics*. This will make them more meaningful to your audience. For instance, you can use *comparisons* to show relationships. Mere numbers have little significance unless they are interpreted in light of the experience and interests of your audience. The following illustration is an example of how incomprehensible figures can be translated into terms that are more easily understood:

> The sun is 92,000,000 miles from the earth. Its diameter is 882,000 miles, or over 100 times larger than the earth. It would take an airplane traveling 250 miles per hour 50 years without stopping to reach the sun.[10]

• *Be sure that their connection with the statistic and the point under discussion is unmistakably clear*. It is not enough that *you* see the relationship between the figures you are using and the idea you are developing. You must be certain that your audience also sees this relationship clearly and recognizes its implications. Take time to establish the connection between your statistics and the point you are making.

• *Present a combination of statistics to emphasize the importance of an issue*. A piling up of different authoritative statistics to illustrate your point can be enormously effective. When using a number of statistical references to support your ideas, it is also important that you present them in an impressive sequence that will culminate in a climax of support for your cause. The following excerpt from a speech by Franklin D. Roosevelt in support of the efficiency of American labor and management illustrates the effective use of this method:

Labor baiters forget that, at our peak, American labor and management have turned out airplanes at the rate of 109,000 per year; tanks, 57,000 per year; combat vessels, 573 per year; landing vessels, 31,000 per year; cargo ships, 19,000,000 tons per year; and small arms ammunition, 23 billion rounds per year.[11]

• *Use visual aids to present statistics.* If your statistics are critical to audience understanding of your main thought, present them by the use of some form of visual aid, such as a chart or graph. Lucas uses a graph to illustrate the fact that statistics about the rise in the divorce rate in America can be more effectively presented visually by a graph than by a recitation of hard-to-remember figures:[12]

If you follow these seven tested and proven guidelines as you do your research for appropriate statistics, you can safely expect that most people will accept the ones you choose as being valid and will be convinced by them.

We have just discussed the value of using visual aids in presenting statistics. Now let's take a look at their further use in public speaking in general. We live in the age of television and multimedia presentations. We have become accustomed to being *shown* by visual communications. Our modern world seems to live by the principle that *seeing* is believing. You will find that visual aids can help you as a speaker in four important ways.

First of all—and probably most important—visual aids can help you gain and hold the *attention* of the audience by arousing their interest in something they can see. People are much more likely to be attentive if they have something to look at. Today, publishers of education books, such as high school and college textbooks, encyclopedias, and even dictionaries, are aware of the effectiveness of visual images. They have kept pace with the modern trend toward the use of the visual by enlivening the pages of their books with drawings, photographs, and maps. You can do the same in your speeches. There is a wide variety of visual aids available for your use. You can choose one or more of the following to draw attention to and to reinforce what you are saying:

- Maps
- Graphs
- Diagrams
- Sketches
- Pictures
- Photographs
- Cartoons
- Films
- Slides
- Overhead transparencies
- Blackboard drawings
- Flip charts
- Models
- Actual objects

The skillful use of one, or perhaps even a combination of these visual aids, will greatly enhance your presentation and will give you a much greater chance of keeping the attention of your audience. And, of course, if you don't have the attention of the audience, you might just as well sit down.

Second, visual aids will provide *clarity* to your presentation. They can help make your meaning clear and, thus, aid audience understanding. Minnick uses the following examples to illustrate how certain visual aids can improve audience understanding of intricate concepts:

> Without charts or pictures it is almost impossible to describe an object that an audience has never seen, such as the middle and inner ear of a human being.
>
> ...if you were trying to explain to an audience how a rotary engine works, you would find your task much easier if you could produce a simple working model of the cylinder of such an engine.[13]

Try to find the visual aid that will most effectively illustrate in visual form what you are trying to convey to your audience in words.

Third, visual aids have the advantage of promoting audience *retention*. They reinforce a message and serve as a strong aid to the memory. The speeches which will stand out most vividly in the minds of your audience will probably be the ones in which there has been the use of some unusual object, interesting specimen, or graphic illustration.

Finally, using visual aids will help by giving you a greater degree of *confidence*. Stage fright is not nearly as likely to overtake you if you have something in visual form to present. You will feel much more at ease if you have a reason for moving about, something to do with your hands, as you point toward or demonstrate your visual aid. You will not feel nearly as conspicuous and alone as you stand before your audience because you will have an ally at your side, in the form of your visual aid, that will serve as a prompter for you and will help you interact with your audience. You will find that your words will come more easily, partly because you will have some relief from the steady gaze of your listeners as you direct their attention toward a model or chart. The increased confidence that you will feel as a result of using a visual aid will certainly make it worth the time and effort that it takes to prepare it.

There are certain things that you should be aware of as you look for and prepare visual materials. Be sure that they fit smoothly and unobtrusively into your presentation and serve simply to illustrate and clarify what you are talking about. Try to choose a visual aid that won't take so much time to present that it will dominate the attention of your audience and cause them to lose sight of your main point. Also, be sure that your visual aid is consistent with the interests and background of your audience—that it is not too technical or complicated for them to understand.

In addition to these considerations, it is important that you choose a visual aid that you are able to present properly. You should know how to operate easily any necessary equipment, such as a motion picture or slide projector. If you feel that you are unable to do this, get someone skilled in using the equipment to operate it for you.

After you have carefully chosen the material that you wish to use in visual form, you should consider the following suggestions in preparing your visual aid for use:

• Be sure that all parts of it (labels, statistics, etc.) are large enough to be seen easily by everyone in the audience.

• Be sure that it is so simple in design that it can be understood almost immediately. (Avoid cluttering it with too many ideas or unnecessary details.)

• Be sure that it is neatly drawn, giving attention to effective use of perspective, color, and appropriate design.

• Mount a chart or picture on a rigid backing, such as poster board, and consider using a colored mat to draw attention to the display.

• Be sure that it is securely attached to a stand or wall so that it does not fall down during your presentation.

• Prepare your visual aid well ahead of time so that you will have time to experiment and be creative.

• Be sure that the proper equipment is available, such as screen, projector, extra bulb, and extension cord.

• Practice using your visual aid. Practice setting up any equipment you may need. Also, Lucas advises, "Run through the entire speech several times, practicing the handling of the aids, the gestures you will make, the timing of each move."[14] The importance of such practice cannot be overemphasized, for if a visual aid is not smoothly and effectively presented, it will be a detriment to your speech instead of an asset.

Now that we have discussed the steps that are necessary for the thorough preparation of visual materials, we need to consider suggestions that will be helpful to you in the actual presentation of the visual aid you have so carefully prepared.

• Explain the visual aid to your audience. State clearly and simply what it means and how it relates to what you are saying. If your listeners don't understand your visual aid, they will only be confused by it.

• Keep your visual aid out of sight until the moment you wish to use it. Then, after you are through with it, put it back out of sight by removing it, covering it, or turning it toward the wall.

• Never stand between your visual aid and the audience, nor turn your back on your audience. Instead, stand to one side of the visual aid and point toward it with a finger, pencil, or pointer, being careful not to block any part of the visual aid with your body.

• Talk to your audience—not to your visual aid—being careful to keep eye contact with your audience while demonstrating your visual aid.

• Avoid long periods of silence when preparing a visual aid. Keep talking to your audience as you set up or take down a display, as you complete a drawing, or as you write on a chalkboard.

• Don't pass out visual materials before or during the course of your speech. They will draw the attention of your listeners away from your message and will cause them to lose track of what you are saying.

It is undeniable that visual aids can be of great benefit to you as a speaker. Lucas observes, "Listeners find a speaker's message more interesting, grasp it more easily, and retain it longer when it is presented visually as well as verbally."[15] Therefore, as you do your research for speech materials, make a conscious effort to look for anything that you could use in visual form, always keeping in mind the limitations imposed on you by your speaking situation. You will find that even the simplest of visual material can be amazingly effective.

CHAPTER 14

GATHERING YOUR MATERIAL

IN ANCIENT times Cicero gave this admonition concerning the responsibility of the public speaker: "It is the duty of the true orator to seek out, hear, read, discuss, handle, and ponder everything that befalls in the life of man, since it is with this that the orator is concerned and this that forms the material with which he has to deal."[1] He was saying quite simply that a speaker has the responsibility of gathering the best and most comprehensive material available to use in preparing to speak to an audience. Although you probably don't consider yourself an orator, you can still heed Cicero's advice. The principle of *thorough preparation* is the same whether you are preparing a major address that could elevate you to the status of an orator or whether you are preparing a simple message for a small club meeting.

It is important that you realize that you will need to gather a wealth of material—far more than you will be able to use. It has been estimated that you should collect four times as much information as you actually need. Obviously, the amount of material you need will be in proportion to the length of time you are required to speak. Keeping this in mind, you should be certain that you have more than enough material to use in filling your time. Then you will not be forced to present irrelevant or inadequate materials—

and thus weaken your effectiveness—simply because you do not have anything better to use. Instead, from the abundance of material you have collected, you will be able to select the very best to use in your speech.

As you approach the task of gathering the material for any presentation, you undoubtedly are aware that such an endeavor will require a great deal of research on your part. You probably also suspect that you should follow some kind of organized plan. Sondel advises us that "there are two stages in the preparation of a speech: (1) At your desk, and (2) On your feet."[2]

Researching your subject falls under the "at your desk" stage. This stage, according to White, should include "thinking, observing, communicating with others and reading."[3] By following these four steps as you do your research, you will be able to discover an amazing amount of material.

You should start first with *yourself*. You will probably be surprised at how much you can contribute to your subject simply by thinking about it. You may discover that you have a large number of very relevant experiences to draw on. After all, you will be bringing to your topic the total of all your experiences–everything that you have learned, read, seen, heard, or felt. By allowing yourself to *think* about your subject, you will find that things which you had long forgotten will surface. Something may occur to you out of a past experience that will give direction to your search for appropriate materials. One expert suggests that you should allow yourself adequate *time* to think:

> Find a quiet, secluded place and, putting aside the haste and pressure of your daily schedule, let your mind roam freely among your thoughts and memories. Place no demands of productivity upon yourself; just meander, or leap, in the track and at the speed that your impulse

directs....The full value of your experiences, former study, backgrounds, and training can only be realized if you *think*.[4]

You should utilize yourself, then, as your first source—through the process of thinking—and gather any information you have in your mind that is relevant to the topic you have chosen.

Next, try to sharpen your powers of *observation,* training yourself to notice things that pertain to your topic. According to Baker and Eubanks, "Observation gives your speech authoritativeness." They comment further, "When you interpret your ideas in terms of direct, personal experience, your audience will place a higher value on what you say."[5]

Be aware that *observing* means more than just physically *seeing* a thing. An observant person is one who is alert to what is going on about her and who makes perceptive judgments about the things she observes. Make a conscious effort to become an accurate, objective observer, and you can be sure that your efforts will result in a greater audience acceptance of what you are saying.

The third step in doing organized research is *communicating with others.* You will find that doing this is one of the best ways to invest your time. You can expect that your investment will yield large dividends in the form of much valuable information that, in many cases, could not be obtained from any other source. As you consider these sources outside of your own thinking and observations, it is important that you try to keep your mind open to *all* the information and points of view available on your topic. You should not discard opinions that are different from your own but should try to be as objective as possible so that the material you collect will be reliable.

If your subject is controversial, consult experts on both sides of the issue. As Minnick states, "You should investigate with an open mind, then, all sides of a controversial topic. Make your research a learning process, not one in which you read selectively to confirm your own opinions."[6] Who knows? Your research might even lead you to adopt a different view of the matter. In any event, to be credible as a speaker, you must at least present other points of view fairly and then express to your audience why your view is different. There is no substitute for objectivity in organizing, interpreting, and evaluating the material you discover in doing your research.

As you can see, communicating with other people who have an interest in or a greater knowledge of your subject is a very important step in the research process. You can consult your friends, people in local businesses and industries, college faculty members, local and national government officials, and experts throughout the nation. But you may wonder how you can utilize their expertise to the fullest. White suggests, "Three methods are available to you for securing information from others: (1) conversation and discussion (2) interviews, and (3) letters."[7]

Informal conversation and discussion can be very helpful in collecting information. Sometimes, even in the course of a social gathering, you can simply turn the conversation toward your speech topic and in so doing gather fresh information and various points of view from those present. In addition to relying on casual social contacts, you can *make* opportunities to discuss your subject with friends, associates, and other people you feel are knowledgeable. One method that you can use is the *interview.*

You may find that a personal interview is a very effective way of securing the information you need. Lucas refers to this kind of interview as a "research" interview. He points out that such an interview is particularly useful in supplying "up-to-the-minute information" and also "information about a fairly narrow subject that might not attract newspaper or other printed coverage." He notes, in addition, that an interview of this type will provide access to "a person who has specialized knowledge about a subject" or to some well-known person whose "viewpoint will add interest and force to your speech."[8]

If you decide to conduct an interview, be aware that there are certain important guidelines that you need to follow:

•*Schedule the interview in advance,* stating the purpose of the interview and why it is important to you. If the person you are to interview is very busy, this advance notice will give that person a chance to set aside a block of uninterrupted time to devote to your interview and will allow your expert time to reflect on the specific information you need.

•*Do adequate advance research in your subject area.* Only then will you have the knowledge and background you need in order to ask meaningful questions. Remember that you should be asking your experts to fill gaps in your own knowledge, not to write your speech for you.

•*Prepare a list of intelligent, specific, pertinent questions.* White advises that you not ask general questions, nor ones that you can easily get from other sources. Instead, he proposes, "Ask for particular data, ideas, judgments."[9] Hobby suggests, "Compose your opening sentence and your closing statement."[10] Doing this will allow you to begin and end the interview smoothly and will conserve valuable time. A smooth beginning, also, will give you the confidence you need to conduct an effective interview. Questions to be avoided, according to Lucas, are those that are leading, hostile, or loaded.[11]

•*Bring with you an appropriate notepad and pen* for taking notes during the interview.

•*Decide whether you want to use a tape recorder.* Of course, you must first, in the course of setting up the interview, obtain permission to use a tape recorder. Many people do not wish to be tape-recorded. However, if the person you are to interview consents to its use, you are then at liberty to weigh the advantages against the disadvantages and decide whether or not to use it.

Two advantages of using a tape recorder, according to Lucas, are: (1) having your hands and mind free of the task of notetaking: and (2) having an altogether accurate record of the interview so that there can be no possible way of forgetting important points or of misquoting your source. Lucas also notes that two *disadvantages* are the fact that: (1) the presence of the tape recorder may cause your subject to be uncomfortable and thus respond in an unnatural way; and (2) you will later have to spend a great deal of time playing the tape to sift out the information, instead of simply writing down the important points during the interview.[12]

•*Be sure to arrive on time and leave on time.* If a length of time for the interview has been designated, adhere strictly to it. If no time limit was set, be alert for signals that your expert wishes to terminate the interview.

•*Conduct yourself in a poised, friendly, and courteous manner.* Bear in mind that the person you are interviewing has granted you a favor and deserves to be treated with respect whether or not you agree with the statements that person is making.

•*Review your notes immediately after the interview* if at all possible. Doing this is important because it will allow you to interpret and organize your notes while they are still fresh on your mind. Next, you should select the material that you think you may be able to use in your speech and transcribe it onto note cards of the same size you are using to record your library research. This will enable you to organize and arrange your interview cards easily with all your other research cards as you prepare to write your speech.

• *Write a letter of appreciation following the interview.* Such a letter is always appropriate and will certainly be welcomed.

Another method of securing information from others is to write letters to them requesting information. Doing this is particularly useful in contacting information services. There are a number of such organizations that have literature that they are eager to distribute. Most libraries have in their reference sections such sources as: the *World Almanac*; the *Trade and Professional Associations of the United States*; and the *Encyclopedia of Associations,* which lists special interest groups in the United States. A listing of government agencies can be obtained from the U.S. Government Printing Office, Washington, D.C. 20402. If you don't know which agency to contact for information pertaining to your particular subject, try writing or calling your congressional representative and request help in finding the right one.

In writing a letter requesting information, first be sure that you allow adequate time to receive an answer. The information you have requested will be useless unless it arrives in time for you to incorporate it in your speech. You will be much more likely to receive a prompt answer if you enclose a stamped, self-addressed envelope. White advises that you *be specific,* stating clearly what information or judgments you need; that you *be brief,* writing only what is necessary; and that you *be businesslike,* but avoid being overly formal.[13]

We have discussed the importance of thinking, observing, and communicating with others while doing your research. Now let's consider the fourth important step in the research process—*reading.* You will find that printed material is the single greatest source of information available to you. We have at our disposal—almost instantly—the accumulated knowledge and cumulative experiences of the whole human race. In fact, you have access to such an incredible array of published material that you will probably have difficulty knowing where to look and what to choose. Your problem will be knowing how to go about tapping this rich resource of past knowledge and, then, how to use it wisely as a foundation to build a bridge to the future.

If you aspire to become outstanding as a speaker, you need to recognize the importance of *general* reading. It will provide a broad background of knowledge that will be invaluable to you in the thinking stage of speech preparation. General reading will, many times, give direction to the reading you will need to do in finding material for a specific speaking assignment. Accordingly, you should make it a habit to read something every day, keeping your mind alert for interesting facts and illustrations. It is a good idea to keep a folder in which you can put notes, ideas, and clippings from your daily reading. You can later go back and separate these random gatherings into categories.

You may feel that general reading is an easy task, but the thought of doing research in a specific area may fill you with dread. Many people tend to slight proper research simply because they do not know how to do it. They feel uncomfortable in a library because they don't know how to use it. Fortunately, learning how to use the library efficiently is a simple matter.

You should turn first to the librarians, who are trained specialists in the field of library use and research. They can be of tremendous help to you and, in most cases, are very friendly and quite willing to assist you in learning how to find what you need quickly and easily. A librarian will be able to instruct you in the use of the *card catalog*, which is essential in locating material in the library. It lists, in alphabetical order, all the books and periodicals contained in the library. A librarian can also instruct you in the use of the *ref-*

erence section of the library, which will put you in touch with an abundance of material in the form of encyclopedias, dictionaries, yearbooks, atlases, biographical guides, and periodical and newspaper indexes.

Don't hesitate to enlist the aid of librarians, not only in learning your way around the library, but also in finding a particular source or a specific bit of information. You will find that using the library becomes easier every time you do it.

As you begin the process of doing library research, do not be tempted to take the easy way out by copying someone else's work and passing it off as your own. This is dishonest and constitutes plagiarism. You can be sure that, sooner or later, you would be found out. At best, you would be terribly embarrassed. At worst, you would be sued. Take whatever time you need to do your own research and form your own evaluations and opinions. Then construct from these a presentation that reflects your own thinking and style.

You may want to take Sondel's advice that, in beginning your research, you should first read articles in periodicals. She states these reasons: "You can read many articles in the time it takes to read one book.... You'll get various opinions about similar problems. This is good because at this stage you are not yet ready to make your own judgments."[14] Then, after you have gained an overall grasp of your topic by reading about it in condensed form, you will be ready to do more detailed reading from other sources.

As you do such specific reading, try to be selective. Obviously, you can't read *everything* pertaining to your subject. Try to choose what appear to be the most important sources. Looking at the title of a book, the author, publisher, and publication date may help you determine how useful that particular book will be to you. Look also at the table of contents, which will reveal what kind of information you can expect to find. Then, if you feel that the book might be helpful to you, flip through it, scanning it to get a better idea of its content. You can later go back and read certain sections more carefully.

As you attempt to sift out and evaluate material, you should make every effort to keep your mind open to new ideas and different opinions. But you should also try to read critically. White observes that many people "tend to worship authority and the printed word." He advises:

> Be skeptical in your reading. Consider whether authors have an axe to grind. Test their reasoning. Examine their evidence. Question their sources. Evaluate carefully their conclusions, not only for their validity but also for their relevance to your purpose. In short, do not be gullible.[15]

Accept or reject information based on the objectivity of its source.

It is very important that you take good, accurate notes as you read and that you carefully record the source, being sure that you have the correct title, author, publication information, and page number. This will save you much time and effort if you later need to go back to that source for any reason.

Be willing to spend whatever time is necessary to do a thorough job in your reading research. Only then will you be able to gather an adequate supply of material to use as you prepare to speak.

After you have gathered your speech materials through the avenues of thinking, observing, communicating with others, and reading, it is time to undertake the task for which you have so long prepared. It is time to begin actually *writing* your speech. Chapter 15 will attempt to guide you as you begin the exciting, but demanding, task of condensing and organizing all the information you have gathered and arranging it into a concise and forceful presentation.

CHAPTER **15**

WRITING YOUR SPEECH

THERE ARE few tasks that require the kind of commitment and self-discipline that is necessary for achieving good writing, and, therefore, good speaking. Good writing demands a high degree of concentration in selecting and organizing the material you have accumulated. It requires that you have the patience to write and rewrite, to edit and revise—even to discard what you have written and start over if you feel that is necessary. It is essential that you have the determination to stick to your writing project until you are satisfied that it is the very best you can make it.

In addition, after you have in written form the makings of an outstanding presentation, you must have the perseverance to practice until your speaking measures up to the high quality of your writing. Then, and then only, can you approach your speaking opportunity with the confidence you need to command attention, to make your point, to sway your audience—indeed, to make a difference.

As a preliminary step, even before you begin the actual writing process, you would do well to hear as many competent public speakers as you can. Note especially the content of their speeches and their presentations, and try to determine what makes them outstanding. You will undoubtedly find that they use effectively many of the elements and techniques that we have discussed in previous chapters. You can benefit greatly from observing the skill with which these experienced speakers use such methods in their speeches. You should listen critically to political speeches, to radio and television news coverage, to speeches at formal and informal occasions. And don't forget that you have ready access to a host of competent speakers in the form of ministers. They are in a constant state of speech preparation, for they must prepare and deliver sermons every week. Take every opportunity that presents itself to observe master speakers, whatever their roles. Hear them, learn from them, and apply what you learn to the writing of your own speech.

As you begin the actual writing process, it is of prime importance that you allow yourself enough time to accomplish your task in an unhurried manner. Good writing usually is not something that can be done quickly, but rather, it requires adequate time for proper reflection, trial and error, the cultivation and refinement of ideas and style.

Your ideas need time to mellow. That is why it is far better to spread your speech preparation over a number of days, or even weeks, instead of trying to cram the whole process into one long session. If you are to produce a piece of writing that rises above the average, you must allow yourself time for the creative process to take place. The writing of your speech is an artistic production that involves the creation of something fresh and new from your own thoughts and research that will be of benefit to your audience.

Because good writing requires you to be creative, don't think that you must go into seclusion and wait for the moment of inspiration to strike. Quite the contrary! The creative process demands a lot of *hard work*. Creativity demands that you work hard in researching your subject and that you work hard writing about it. Lucas estimates that "Most people speak at an average rate of roughly 120–150 words a minute. This means that a six-minute speech will consist of roughly 720–900 words."[1] Using these figures as a guide, you must be certain that you gather enough information to use in filling your time with fresh, meaningful material.

As you actually settle down to the task of composing your speech, you should keep your topic always in the back of your mind. Use every possible opportunity to think about it—while driving to work, while waiting at a traffic light, while washing dishes. Utilize any time—however brief—when you can focus your mind on your topic. You don't have to be seated at your desk to think and to organize.

This continuous awareness of your speech project will serve you well. You will be surprised at how many ideas will come to you just in the course of your everyday activities if you allow your subconscious to take over and work for you even when your mind is not actively engaged in thinking about your speech. Experts in the study of the mind believe that your subconscious mind works for you even while you are asleep. You may wake up and suddenly an idea or phrase that has previously eluded you will pop into your head. Your speech will be enriched by the use of this sudden bit of inspiration.

When these flashes of inspiration come, it is very important that you write them down immediately—even if it means getting out of bed in the middle of the night. Inspiration can be of short duration, and your memory of it may be fleeting. If you don't capture in writing an idea or a skillful wording while it is still fresh on your mind, it may be gone forever. You may not be able to remember it even a few minutes later. Then, before you settle down to the task of writing your speech, you can go back and organize all these random thoughts, ideas, and phrasings and categorize them so that you can find them easily. Later on, you can refine them as you weave them into your speech.

Before you begin the actual writing of your speech, you should be aware that self-discipline is essential to the writing process. You must force yourself to write, even if you feel you can't. It is only through a trial and error process that good writing can be achieved. The only way you can improve your writing is to write, rewrite, and revise what you have written; but you can be sure that improvement will come. At times it may seem that you are forced to proceed at a tortoise-like pace—that appropriate words are won only after great struggle. But be patient. You may have a sudden burst of inspiration that will loose your words and cause them to flow with such ease that you will be astonished at the brilliance of your own writing.

As important as it is to stick to your writing project with determination, you need to be aware that sometimes the best way to proceed is to stop. Creativity cannot always be commanded, nor can a high level of creativity be maintained indefinitely. It is certainly true that the actual process of writing itself fosters and nurtures creativity, but there will be times when you reach a stalemate as you strive to capture creativity.

When your thinking becomes dull, when you are unable to concentrate, to organize, you need to take a break. It is time to let your writing rest for a while–maybe even quit for the day. Relax and let your mind refresh itself. Perhaps tomorrow, when you reread your material, miraculously, the thoughts which refused to come today will flow readily.

We have discussed certain preliminary steps that you need to take before you begin actually drafting your speech. We have also discussed how to prepare yourself mentally for your task. Now, we need to get down to specifics. We need to talk about where to start and, then, how to proceed in the orderly development of a concise, forceful, and effective presentation.

GUIDELINES FOR SPEECH WRITING

• Be sure that what you say is worth something to that particular audience—that it *matters* to them. Tailor your speech to fit your listeners' needs and provide something worthwhile for them.

• Be sure that your speech has a goal. Dr. David Campbell wrote a book entitled *If you don't know where you are going, you'll probably end up somewhere else.*[2] This is certainly true of speech-making. If you end up somewhere else, of course, so will your audience. Be sure that your audience is clearly aware of your goal. Sondel instructs us: "*State your purpose.* Don't assume that a listener knows where you come in on the deal. Tell him. In plain words."[3]

• Don't deal in general ideas. Be specific. Tell how something will affect your particular audience. Maybe mention someone in the audience by name or give a hypothetical illustration involving members of the audience.

• Use the same tact and good manners in your speech that you would use in your daily social contacts. Never use your speaking situation as an opportunity to be abusive in any way.

• Be sure that your treatment of your material is fresh and new—something that your listeners are not likely to have heard before.

• Be careful to vary your illustrations so that they will appeal, as White suggests, to "people on various economic, social and intellectual levels, with a correspondingly wide range of interests, attitudes and experiences."[4]

• Use stories as illustrations. A story will be remembered much more easily than dry facts or statistics.

• Use repetition to reinforce audience understanding of your main points. Don't repeat word for word, but vary the wording of your ideas as you weave repetition into your

182 BASIC MEETING MANUAL

speech. (Sometimes, however, it is effective to repeat the same phrase for emphasis.) White offers this suggestion: "Important names, dates, and figures should be repeated at least once....Important ideas should probably be repeated at least twice."[5]

• Simplify difficult or complicated material that is beyond the background and experience of your audience. Explain technical material. Reword it using simpler words, or provide an illustration that will clarify it. In doing this, however, *never* be condescending toward your audience.

• Be cautious in using humor. Humor can be very effective in providing a change of pace and in establishing good rapport with your audience, but you must be wary in using it. Use humor only if it can be woven naturally into your speech—if it has a purpose—and only if you know that you can use it well. Use only stories that can be told in good taste anywhere and at any time. Also, don't ever be humorous at the expense of another. You should be aware that humor is more than stories, puns, and anecdotes. White observes:

> Sparkling, original humor can be found in a witty turn of phrase, in mimicry, in a clever bit of repartee with the chairman, in hyperbole or understatement, in a pointed reference to some aspect of the occasion or speech situation, in a touch of irony, in a ridiculous comparison or contrast, in an unexpected twist to a familiar quotation or poem, and so on.[6]

One final word about humor: don't overuse it and become a clown; in doing so, you may keep your audience from taking you seriously.

• Avoid using clichés, trite sayings, and newly coined words.

• Don't overload your speech with information. Proodian

advises, "Offer a few choice nuggets. New information is retained in small quantities. So be selective."[7]

• Try to use some personal material in your speech. This gives your listeners a chance to know you better and tends to establish a friendly rapport with them.

• Use all of your time for yourself. Don't spend your speaking time refuting someone else's ideas or opinions.

• Be sure that you put quotation marks around direct quotations in your written speech and that you acknowledge the source. It is also important to use material in the context intended by the author. It would be unethical to quote material to prove a point that is inconsistent with what the author intended.

• Keep your speech brief and well within the time limit. A long, rambling speech is one that lacks adequate preparation. Such a speech needs to be condensed and refined. As the old adage states, it is quality, not quantity, that is important.

• Be sure that your speech is free of obvious grammatical errors. Such errors are very distracting to your audience and will diminish your effectiveness. If you don't feel competent in grammar, have someone who is knowledgeable edit your speech for you.

Keep these suggestions firmly in mind while you undertake the next step in your speech preparation—that of constructing the all-important outline. Just as the navigator needs instruments to keep his ship on course, so the speaker needs some means of keeping his speech on course. The outline is that instrument needed by the speaker.

Be sure that your outline covers your subject, that all parts of it hang together, and that one part of it flows logically into the next, leading clearly to your conclusion. Such an outline, according to Spicer, will "enable you to make speeches which audiences may not always agree with, but which they will understand, respect, and remember."[8] And, if you gain the understanding and respect of your audience and imprint your thoughts on their minds, you have succeeded as their speaker.

As you begin the task of making your outline, first arrange all your note cards into categories. You will need a large desk or table for spreading out the cards so that you will have easy access to all of them. Then, drawing from these materials, jot down a list of the thoughts and ideas that you feel are the most important and that you want to include in your speech. This list might even include as many as forty or fifty items. It is from this list that you will be able to develop the outline that you will use in writing the rough draft of your speech.

Since a good outline is essential to good writing, and thus to good speaking, we need to consider some practical suggestions for making an effective outline.

• First, write out one sentence that states the purpose of your speech and what you hope to accomplish by it. Keep this sentence before you as you compose your outline.

• Use a standard system of symbols and indentations. Indicate the major headings or main points of your speech with Roman numerals, the subheadings with capital letters, further subheadings with Arabic numerals, and still further subheadings with lower-case letters. This will give a stairstep effect which makes your outline clear and easy to follow, as you can see from the following illustration:

   I. Major Heading
       A. Subheading
       B. Subheading
           1. Sub-subheading
           2. Sub-subheading

    a. Sub-sub-subheading
    b. Sub-sub-subheading

• Choose at least two, but no more than five, major headings. Having more than five indicates that you have not spent enough time condensing and organizing your material. Too many main points will make it difficult for your audience to understand and remember your message.

• Be sure that the following six things are true of your major headings (main points):

1) The major headings should cover all the essential points of your topic.

2) Each major heading should be directly related to your topic and should be a logical division of it.

3) Each major heading should be a separate thought, independent of the other headings.

4) Each major heading should be of the same importance as the other headings.

5) Each major heading should be phrased in the same grammatical structure as the others.

6) The major headings should be progressive, leading your audience in a logical way to your conclusion.

• Apply the same six guidelines in selecting your subheadings that you used in selecting your major headings. These subheadings serve as explanations of the main headings and may include such things as quotations, illustrations, logical reasoning, and visual aids.

If you study these suggestions and then carefully prepare your outline using them as guidelines, you will already be well under way in the task of writing the rough draft of your speech. You will have in abbreviated form what you want to say. Now all you have to do is fill in the details and add the supporting material.

Before we continue our discussion of the writing of your rough draft, we should point out that some speech experts feel that a good outline is all that you need for speaking. They feel that your speech will be more natural and spontaneous if you do not write it out. They recommend that you become thoroughly familiar with your outline and then choose your words as you go along, just as you would in conversation.

Other authorities feel that writing out your speech is essential to good speaking. They believe that it is only by writing out your speech that you can refine it and shape it to fit most effectively into your allotted speaking time. They believe that writing your speech allows you to choose carefully the most effective wording and gives you confidence in knowing that you will not have to fumble around for words. Writing out your speech does not mean that you should read your speech word for word. It simply gives you the opportunity of controlling more effectively what you will say.

If you choose to write out your speech, you need to give some attention to your writing (and, thus, speaking) *style*. It is important for your style to reflect your own personality. Hobby advises, "Don't try to imitate someone else's style. Be yourself. Be natural."[9] Try to develop your own style by choosing words that are natural for you to use and that reflect your own personality, but which will also satisfy the requirements of the public speaking situation.

As you begin writing the rough draft of your speech, you should first refer back to the one sentence that you wrote out before you started constructing your outline—the one that stated the purpose of your speech and what you hope to accomplish by it. Keep this sentence and your outline before you while you are writing.

Be sure that you say enough to make your point convincingly, but don't just talk to fill the time or to impress your audience with your superior knowledge. Try to choose only the things that are relevant and forceful and that cause your speech to advance. Keep your style simple and direct. Choose only the things that *can't* be left out—that are useful to your purpose.

You should give a lot of thought to the words you use in your speech, since it is your choice of words that will make the difference between a dull speech and a dynamic one. McFarland makes this comment on the importance of words:

> No idea ever takes the form of achievement until after it has been formed into words. Whether a man builds a temple, or dashes himself and his fellowman to death over a precipice, depends solely upon what words he believes. Through words we decide whether to pray for our fellowman or to prey on them [sic], whether to follow our leaders or murder them.[10]

You can see, then, that it is important to choose your words carefully. Hobby recommends that you use simple, forceful words because such words are more easily pronounced, more easily heard and understood, and are just as powerful as big words.[11]

It is important to find the *one* most effective word and use it instead of using several words that express the same idea. Try to use vivid words that paint pictures—that cause your listeners to see, hear, smell, taste, and feel. Using such words greatly increases the chance that your audience will understand and remember what you say and thus be influenced by it.

In writing your rough draft keep always in mind that you need to vary your writing style. Don't let it become monotonously the same. Instead, as Sondel advises, "Use changes in timing—choppy, smooth, pauses, etc. Use changes in tempo....Use changes in color....Use changes of pitch."[12] Use some short sentences and some longer ones to provide variety. However, don't ever use a sentence that is so long and involved that your audience is unable to follow your thought. Although there may be times when a longer sentence is needed, it is generally better to follow Hobby's advice: "A good rule of thumb is, if there are more than 20 words the sentence may either be rewritten or divided into two shorter ones."[13]

After you have carefully prepared the rough draft of the main body of your speech, you need to give the same careful attention to writing your introduction and your conclusion. These two elements are of great importance to your success as a speaker. Spicer tells us, "First and last impressions are critical."[14] He emphasizes the importance of a good beginning and ending by saying that "as long as you start and end stylishly, and convey some semblance of orderly thought in the body of your talk, 90 percent of any given audience will be convinced that you've pulled off a first-rate speech."[15]

White estimates that the introduction should be perhaps 10 percent of the length of the speech. He states that it "may serve two functions: to stimulate favorable interest in you as the speaker and in your message, and to orient the listeners to the nature and purpose of the Body."[16] He lists several ways that you can gain the favorable attention of your audience. He suggests that you can begin your speech by "referring to the significance of the subject, telling an illustrative story, using a stimulating quotation, or mentioning common bonds, such as experiences, interests, or attitudes, that you share with the listeners."[17] Sondel believes that you should be able to state your objective to your audience in just one sentence: "We understand what we hear only when we can sum it up in one sentence."[18] Sondel believes that it is also important to tell your audience why you are speaking on your topic: "It is important to say why. People want to know something about your motives. If you don't tell them, they'll have to guess, and they may guess wrong. It may be wise also to tell why they should listen."[19]

Proodian suggests another approach for getting off to a good start. He advises that you resist "the natural instinct to save the best for last. Start with your humdinger. Pull your best idea out of the body of your speech and use it at the very start. You can develop it later in its normal setting. Strong ideas can always be repeated as a means of emphasis."[20]

Whichever approach you choose to use, the important thing is that your introduction should tell your audience briefly what they can expect to hear and should arouse their interest so that they will want to hear it.

Hobby uses the following illustration to point up the importance of continuing to make your audience aware of what you want them to remember:

An old preacher explained, "First, I tell them what I am going to tell them."

"Then, I tell them."

"Finally, I tell them what I told them."[21]

The importance of an effective conclusion cannot be overemphasized. It gives you one last chance to make your point, to repeat what you have been trying to say, to tie it all together. An effective conclusion will be brief, but to the point. A lengthy, weak conclusion can destroy the impact of an otherwise outstanding presentation. White suggests that your conclusion be no longer that 5 percent of your total speech length and that it "restate the point of the speech, list or review concisely the main ideas of the Body, and/or summarize indirectly with a quotation, comparison, or example."[22]

Above all, be sure that your conclusion is forceful. Even while you are doing research and while you are writing the main body of your speech, you should keep your eyes open for material that you can use in making a dynamic conclusion. Spend whatever time it takes to word your conclusion effectively, then become so thoroughly familiar with it that you won't have to lose eye contact with your audience by referring to your notes. If you prepare your conclusion carefully and then memorize it, you will be able to deliver it confidently, flawlessly, and with feeling.

After you have finished writing the rough draft of your entire speech, you will be ready for the final step in your writing process—that of editing. Just as the process of refining improves the quality of steel, so the process of refining your speech, through editing, will improve its quality. There are specific things you should look for as you edit your speech. Spicer offers this advice: "In editing your copy take out any word or phrase that does not lead to directness, clarity, or simplicity."[23] Take out anything that is weak or irrelevant. Be sure that one part of your speech leads directly to the next.

It is also important that your speech be edited for correct grammar, punctuation, and spelling, even though your listeners will not be aware of your spelling and punctuation. Hobby observes, "You will speak better from a well-edited text. Also, someday someone will read what you have written, or maybe you too will write a book."[24]

The time you spend editing your speech will not be time wasted. On the contrary! While you are making your speech more and more effective, you will become more and more familiar with its content. In a sense, you will already be practicing your speech, and practicing is absolutely essential to good speaking. Chapter 16 will provide some helpful suggestions for perfecting your presentation by practicing.

PRACTICING YOUR SPEECH

BY THE time you are ready to practice your speech, you will have devoted a great deal of time and effort to research, to writing your rough draft, and to editing and perfecting that rough draft into the finished copy. The time has now come to practice so that you can effectively transform your silent masterpiece into a vital presentation worthy of the time and effort you have expended in creating it.

You may feel inadequate as you approach the task of delivering your speech, but you can be comforted by knowing that through diligent practice, you can create that special chemistry between yourself and your audience that is so necessary for effective speaking.

As you begin practicing your speech, you need to be aware that you are not practicing to achieve some artificial standard, nor to imitate some outstanding speaker. You are practicing so that you can best present yourself and your viewpoint through the medium of your prepared speech, which should itself reflect your own individuality. You should deliver your speech in a way that is consistent with your personality. Remember that no two of us are alike. A speaking style that is effective for another speaker may be artificial for you. Therefore, determine at the very beginning that you will make every effort to project your own personality to your audience so that you will appear genuine. If you are genuine, you will be able to establish a good relationship with your audience.

It is through practicing your speech that you will acquire skill in communicating with your audience. *Skill* is the key to success in speaking, and *practice* is the key to speaking skillfully. Let's consider, therefore, some suggestions that will be helpful to you as you begin practicing your speech.

• Practice good speech habits in your everyday speech so that your public speaking will be correct. You should evaluate your speech habits and, as Sondel advises, "Take stock. And then go into training. Watch your enunciation, your grammar....If you want to be yourself—at your best—when in company, watch your everyday speech habits. Or else!"[1]

• Practice reading aloud. Read anything—the newspaper, a book or magazine. This will allow you to become accustomed to hearing your own voice, then you won't be distracted by it when you are delivering your speech.

• Do not memorize your opening sentence. Have firmly in mind, in a general way, what you want to say, but allow yourself the flexibility of responding to an introduction or some comment or of adjusting to some unexpected situation.

• Don't try to memorize your entire speech. If you do, it will probably sound "canned" and unnatural. Also, the least distraction—and there will probably be many—could throw you off course. Do memorize your outline. Then, if you become distracted, you will be able to reconstruct your thoughts and choose words suitable for the occasion, even if they are not the words you had planned to use. Practice until you are thoroughly familiar with your outline, perhaps varying the wording each time. This will allow for a certain amount of flexibility.

• Use a felt-tipped colored marker to highlight key words and phrases in the outline of your speech. This will allow you to pick them out easily as you glance at your notes while you are speaking.

• Don't hesitate to use notes. In regard to using notes, Hobby observes, "Don't be afraid to use notes. It is better than forgetting what to say. Notes are not a sign of weakness, rather they are proof of preparation, especially for a nonprofessional speaker."[2] You should, however, try to minimize the use of visible notes by practicing until you can glance at your highlighted notes without calling attention to the fact that you are referring to them.

• Time yourself when you are practicing. Then, if you find that your speech is too short, you can add more pertinent information to lengthen it. If it is too long, you can trim it down, leaving out the less important details. Also, timing yourself will allow you to practice maintaining the momentum of your speech so that you won't have to speed up at the end in order to finish on time.

• In delivering your speech, when you have finished one idea and are getting ready for the next, simply pause. Don't clutter your pauses with "uhs" or "ahs." A pause allows your listeners to catch up with your thinking, and it allows you time to think before moving on to your next point. It also gives you time to readjust your posture or to move to the side of the lectern.

• After you have practiced a few times, make a tape recording of your speech. Then play it back, and you will hear yourself as others hear you. As Hobby observes, "Unfortunately for most of us, the recorder is like the camera, brutally truthful."[3] He notes, however, that a recording will be very helpful to you as you try to improve your speech habits: "While you listen you can evaluate your speech habits and diction. Be impartial and analytical, if you can."[4]

• Try to eliminate from your speech what Hobby calls "time stallers." Hobby counsels, "Anyone who wishes to improve speaking ability can make a long stride toward doing so by reducing or eliminating the urhs, ahs, and-ers, and the you-knows."[5] He notes that they are used by many speakers "to let their minds catch up with their mouths."[6] When you record your speech, you can count the "ahs" and try to eliminate, or at least reduce them, the next time you record your speech.

• Try to adjust the pace of your speech to the difficulty of the material you are presenting. Breeze through it when it's easy; slow down when it gets heavy.

• If you are using humor, you need to keep in mind that telling a humorous story well is a fine art. You will need to practice a lot if you are to do it effectively. Practice especially your timing, since it is essential to good storytelling. Also, it is a good idea to write down the exact wording of the punch line so that you won't bungle it. Hobby suggests: "Don't laugh while you are telling a story, or advertise it before telling it."[7] Try to evaluate objectively whether you are doing a good job. If your audience doesn't laugh at your jokes, don't tell them.

• If, as an inexperienced speaker, you do not feel comfortable speaking from notes only, then don't hesitate to read your speech. If you decide to read it, be sure that you practice until you can read it naturally and easily.

• Practice using your visual aids so that you can use them effectively and can know how much time it takes to present them. You will find that using visual aids will relieve your nervousness.

• Try to anticipate any situation that may arise in your speaking situation. If there is a microphone and you aren't prepared to use one, if there is no lectern to hold your notes—any unexpected circumstance can be very unsettling.

Try to find out what to expect, and then practice taking everything into consideration.

As we conclude our discussion of practicing your speech, we need to give some special attention to using a microphone properly. A microphone is a great help when used properly, a great hindrance when used incompetently. If it is at all possible, you should practice your speech before the microphone you will be using. If this is not possible, then practice using a makeshift microphone. Hobby makes this suggestion:

> Practice at home as though you are addressing the auditorium microphone....On the surface in front of you, place a tall glass or a book on end with a pen or pencil balanced on top. Pretend that the object in front of you is the microphone and that the audience is beyond the table or desk. Practice moving around it to scan the audience....and talk into the pen or pencil....It is a lot better to feel foolish at home alone, and get over it, than to be embarrassed in front of a crowd![8]

As you practice your speech, using an actual microphone or one that you have contrived, there are a number of things that you need to keep in mind. You will find that the following suggestions, drawn from Hobby's discussion of the proper use of a microphone, will be helpful to you:

• Adjust the height of the microphone so that it will be below your mouth and pointed upward toward you.

• If you are using a clip-on microphone, adjust your voice volume so that it picks up properly.

• If you are using a hand-held microphone, hold it six to eight inches away from your mouth—or at a distance that allows your audience to hear comfortably.

• Have a friend sit or stand at the back of the auditorium

and give you some kind of prearranged signal to indicate whether you should raise your voice or lower it.

• Make an effort to use a pleasant voice—one that is not harsh, strident, grating, or nasal.

• Speak clearly and distinctly into the microphone.

• Don't let your voice drop toward the end of a sentence.

• Don't shout into the microphone.

• If you are emphasizing a point by speaking more loudly, back away from the microphone; if you are lowering your voice, lean closer to the microphone.

• Don't move your head back and forth like an oscillating fan, but move your head and your body together from one side to the other, always being careful to face the microphone.

• Don't rattle papers, jingle coins, tap your foot, or strike the lectern.

• Above all, direct your voice waves toward the microphone.

Although you should practice as many speaking techniques as you can, it is impossible to anticipate all aspects of your speaking situation. You simply have to adjust to them as they arise. Chapter 17 will provide suggestions for adjusting to your speaking situation while you are presenting your speech.

CHAPTER 17

PRESENTING YOUR SPEECH

LET'S SUPPOSE that the moment for which you have so diligently prepared has finally arrived. You have completed all the necessary steps in preparing your speech. You have practiced until you feel comfortable with your material. You know that you have something worthwhile to say, and in the privacy of your home or office, you feel that you can deliver it rather well. But you realize that you must shortly stand before an audience and make that same presentation that you have practiced so faithfully. It is now that your old enemy, stage fright, begins to resurface. You must, at this time, fortify yourself by remembering certain things that will lessen your apprehension and allow you to make a credible, maybe even brilliant, presentation.

First of all you need to remember that most of your audience could not do as well as you will do, and many would not even attempt it. Be comforted by Spicer's assessment of your audience:

> The terror of bombing in public is so universal that 90 percent of any audience (the really "unaccustomed to public speaking") look on any decent stump speaker as a practitioner of black magic. If you can play such a magician plausibly, you will pass—forgive me—for somebody even smarter than you are.[1]

There might be someone out there in that silent majority who could do a better job than you are doing—if they had the nerve to try. What makes you a cut above them is that you have had the courage to do it! You have made adequate preparation. You have done your homework. You know more about your subject than your audience does. They are waiting for you to inform them. As McFarland comments:

> It should be remembered that people speak because they were *invited* to speak. If you are the person so invited, it means that someone in authority wanted to hear what you had to say.[2]

You can feel confident knowing that you will be helping your audience by sharing your knowledge with them and that they will probably be receptive to your efforts.

Remember, also, that stage fright, as Baxter notes, "is a guarantee that you will not make a dull, listless speech." He reminds us: "The very best speakers continue to feel such a stimulus even after years of experience, and they derive from it an urge and a zest that keeps them from being listless and apathetic."[3] Spicer insists: "You can master the negative tension by channeling it as a positive force."[4] And channel it you must, for if you appear to be nervous or agitated, you will transmit this feeling to your audience and make them also feel uncomfortable and embarrassed.

White offers this reassurance: "You appear more confident than you feel. Be assured that butterflies are usually undetectable, muscle tremor is so minute it is unnoticable in most cases, and only a surgeon sees a racing heart."[5] In all likelihood, then, on the outside you will appear calm and self-assured even though you are a nervous wreck inside.

Since it is *visible* nervousness that is detrimental to your effectiveness, we need to consider some things that will help you control it.

First of all, before you leave for your speaking engagement, you should give careful attention to your clothes and grooming. A good appearance is important in making a favorable impression on your audience. Also, you will feel more confident if you know that you are appropriately dressed and neatly groomed.

Next, review your speech so that it will be fresh on your mind. Then, as Hobby counsels, "On the way tell yourself 'This is going to be my best so far. I am going to help everyone there'....After all you know more about what you are going to say than anyone else."[6]

If you could speak immediately after you arrive, you would be a lot less likely to become agitated. But, unfortunately, this is rarely possible. As Sondel comments, "If you could arrive on the scene and snap right into your speech, maybe you'd be all right. But ten to one you'll have to pretend to eat something or listen to reports and...to a singer and last month's minutes."[7] During this waiting period, keep reminding yourself of Sondel's comment, "The excitement we feel is essential to performance."[8]

While you are awaiting your turn to speak, make a conscious effort to listen carefully to the comments of those who precede you. Come prepared to jot down a few notes so that you will have something to refer to later if you wish to comment on something you heard. You will find that listening and taking notes will give you a chance to expend some of your pent-up nervous energy.

If you feel extremely up-tight, follow Hobby's advice and make yourself yawn by pressing the forefinger edge of your hand to your throat just below your chin. Then, "With your throat muscles push against your hand. THINK YAWN. Try it. It works. This exercise relaxes the muscles of your throat. Your voice will sound less strained."[9]

Baxter suggests another technique that will help you relax: "Deep and regular breathing while you are still seated and after you have begun to speak is another very valuable practice."[10] He suggests, also: "Consciously think of relaxing the muscles of the body. Mind has much influence over muscle."[11]

Now, finally, the time has come for you to speak. The room grows silent, your audience is attentive, and your heart is pounding. You know that first impressions are extremely important. Hobby relates, "It has been said that you have ten (10) seconds to make a good first impression and ten words to get the attention of your audience."[12] Even as you approach the speaker's platform, you should consciously try to present yourself in the best possible way. Baxter makes this suggestion:

> When walking to the platform, walk so as to create confidence; walk as one who knows where he is going and why he is going there. Neither hurry nor lag, but take your position as one who has a right to be there.[13]

After you reach the lectern, stand up straight and try to project warmth and friendliness to your audience. Be enthusiastic about speaking before them. Your enthusiasm will be infectious, and they will be glad you are there. Smile at your audience, and while you are smiling, look at their faces—establish eye contact.

Eye contact is all-important to effective speaking. Hobby comments, "Looking at the people you are talking to opens the door to communications. A look and a smile is like a handshake—a form of personal contact....It is a silent way of saying, 'I am talking to you.' "[14]

Now that you are ready to speak your first words, be sure that you speak loudly enough for the people in the back row to hear easily.

While you are delivering your speech, you should keep in

mind certain do's and dont's that experienced speakers have found to be helpful:

• Acknowledge your introduction graciously. Never correct some small mistake that was made about you. Hobby proposes this as a proper way to acknowledge your introduction and to begin your speech:

> Thank you (name and title of the one who introduced you). Ladies and gentlemen, or fellow lodge, or club members. (If notables are at the speaker's table or in the audience, recognize them before greeting the audience).[15]

Never begin by apologizing. As Proodian notes:

> If you confess how "unaccustomed" or "uneasy" you are as a speaker, you divert attention from your topic to yourself. The audience should always be confident of you as the speaker because, whether you wish it or not, you are for that moment in charge."[16]

• Be aware that to be effective you must adjust to your particular speaking situation. Hobby suggests that you may need to "vary your presentation or attitude if you see doubt or uncertainty" reflected by your listeners and that you may need "to repeat, clarify, or explain a particular point before proceeding."[17]

• Establish and maintain eye contact with your audience. Sondel recommends, "Find a pair of interesting eyes and speak directly to one person—just as you would in conversation. Hold tight until you finish an idea. Then seek new eyes."[18] Choose someone who is alert and attentive and who is interacting and responding to your message. Such a person will be invaluable to you as you attempt to adjust your comments and delivery to your audience.

- Concentrate on your subject and your audience—not on yourself.
- Don't try to think about what you will say next while you are still speaking on another thought. As Sondel observes, "Thinking about two ideas at once takes two heads. There is only one way to keep going intelligently and that is to stay with your *present* thought....When you come to the end of that thought, stop. Wait. What comes next?...You can't miss."[19]
- If you are presenting an exact quotation, quote it verbatim. If you are simply paraphrasing, then tell the audience so. White suggests this as the proper method of presenting a quotation:

> Avoid using the words "quote" and "end of quotation" unless it is exceedingly important that the listeners know exactly which words belong to your source. Ordinarily, let a change of pitch, rate or emphasis indicate the beginning and ending of a quotation.[20]

- Don't thump or pound the lectern.
- Don't put one foot in a chair.
- Don't pace about.
- Don't put your hands in your pockets. Instead, keep your hands loosely at your sides. Then, if you want to make a gesture of some kind, you can do so naturally. It is very important that your gestures look natural—not contrived. Using suitable gestures and body movements will help you speak more effectively and will help relieve your nervousness.
- Don't become flustered if you make a mistake. It is inevitable that sooner or later you will goof while speaking. But, as Lucas comments, "Even if you do make a mistake during a speech, that is no catastrophe."[21] He believes that making a mistake only makes you seem more human. Hobby offers this advice on how to recover from a mistake:

You may continue as if not conscious of your error. If it is not important this may be better. You can 'go back around.' This lets you restate the issue giving the correct word, figure, or statement; also this shows that you know what you should have said.[22]

Sometimes you can simply make a joke of your mistake. Having a sense of humor is very important in public speaking. According to Hobby, "A sense of humor keeps you from taking yourself too seriously. It frees you to laughing with others when you have goofed. It keeps you from feeling embarrassed or humiliated."[23]

• Always be courteous to your audience, no matter what. Respond graciously and appreciatively. As Hobby advises, "If the response is hostile, cold or neutral, be pleasant anyway. You did the best you could, so have no regrets."[24]

It is indeed important that you have "no regrets" after you have made your best effort in presenting your speech. If the results were not as outstanding as you would have wished, don't abandon ship. You can expect smoother sailing next time. Lucas makes this observation, "Learning to give a speech is not much different from learning any other skill— it proceeds by trial and error."[25] You can be comforted by knowing that Beethoven's first composition wasn't a symphony. Van Cliburn's first recital piece wasn't a concerto. Paul Harvey's first speech wasn't on a national radio network. It is only by repeatedly speaking in public that improvement will come. But, it *will* come, and it will be progressive.

McFarland offers this encouragement:

Babe Ruth hit 714 home runs in his big-league career. Everyone knows that record. But he made another big-league record. He struck out 1330 times. People remember him as the home-run king because he *kept swinging*.[26]

If you "keep swinging," Lucas promises that "your fears about public speaking will gradually recede until they are replaced by only a healthy nervousness before you rise to speak."[27] If you "keep swinging," every speech will be better than the last. If you "keep swinging," your words will "inspire your audience because you will offer something of worth, and you will become able to speak clearly, fluently, and persuasively in any situation that requires you to speak in public. Indeed, you will have reached that goal most desired by any public speaker—the ability to make a difference!

PART THREE:

GUIDELINES
AND SAMPLES FOR
SPECIFIC
SPEAKING SITUATIONS

CHAPTER **18**

LEADING THE PLEDGE OF ALLEGIANCE TO THE FLAG

IF YOU are called upon to lead the Pledge of Allegiance to the Flag, protocol requires a simple two-step process.[1] First, enlist the group's participation by saying, "Please join me in pledging allegiance to the Flag of our country," or "Please join me in pledging allegiance to the Flag of the United States of America."

Then, turn and face the Flag, wherever it is displayed. If you are a civilian, stand at attention and place your right hand over your heart while repeating the pledge; if you are in the military, salute the Flag while repeating the pledge:

> I pledge allegiance to the Flag of the United States of America and to the Republic for which it stands, one Nation under God, indivisible, with liberty and justice for all.

The proper way to display the Flag indoors is as follows:

• When displaying the Flag indoors with another flag, the Flag of the United States will be on the right with its staff crossing over the staff of the other flag.

• If the Flag is displayed flat on the speaker's platform, it should be placed behind and above the speaker with the union to the speaker's right.

• When flown from a staff in a church chancel or speaker's platform, the Flag should be placed on the speaker's right. If placed elsewhere than on the platform, it should be on the right of the audience as they face the platform.

• The National Flag should be placed in the center, and higher, when displayed with a group of state, local or organizational flags flown from staffs.

CHAPTER 19

INTRODUCING A SPEAKER

IF YOU are introducing a speaker at a gathering of any kind, your role will be to pave the way for your speaker by building respect, creating good will, and arousing interest in the subject to be discussed. Your message to the audience should be that you are presenting a speaker whom they will greatly enjoy. Then, briefly, tell them why.

Your first responsibility is to gain the attention of the audience, who may be engaged in conversations with each other at the time you begin your introduction. If you are skillful, you will gain and hold their attention so that the speaker may rise to address an attentive and receptive audience.

In order to prepare an effective introduction, follow these guidelines:

• Be brief. Don't infringe on your speaker's time. Usually two to three minutes is long enough for a speech of introduction. It may be even shorter if the speaker is prominent. In general, the more prominent the speaker, the shorter the introduction. Remember, your task is to focus attention on the main speaker, not on yourself.

• Show that the speaker is qualified to speak on the selected topic by describing educational background and major accomplishments and by mentioning any honors or positions of trust held by the speaker. Request in advance a copy of the speaker's biography, which will usually include education, degrees, military service, positions of responsibility, honors, club membership, and places of residence.

• Give the speaker's name accurately. Be sure that you know how to pronounce it correctly.

• Announce the speaker's subject, but don't discuss it at all. Leave that to your speaker.

• Say something that makes the speaker seem human. Perhaps tell something about the speaker's family, hobbies, or philosophy of life. Use the testimony of friends or tell an incident from the speaker's life that will reveal character or a sense of humor.

• Check with the speaker beforehand to be certain that your introductory remarks are accurate.

• Never say anything that could be embarrassing to the speaker.

• Don't overpraise the speaker and thus lead the audience to expect too much. Give due credit, but don't embarrass the speaker by excessive, unwarranted flattery.

• Be sure that the tone of your introduction fits the formality of the occasion. If the occasion is an informal business meeting, your introduction should be more casual than an introduction at a formal banquet.

The following techniques will contribute to an effective introduction:

• Look at the audience when you begin your introduction, and continue looking at them until you finish pronouncing the speaker's name clearly, distinctly, and loudly enough to be heard by anyone in the audience.

• In delivering your introduction, be sincere, enthusiastic, gracious, and welcoming.

- In your concluding statements repeat the speaker's name and the speech title.
- Turn and look toward the speaker after (and only after) you have completed your introduction. Then, gesture toward the speaker, and lead the audience in applause if appropriate. If the speaker is of great prominence, make a gesture for the audience to rise as the speaker comes to the platform.
- Don't turn your back as you announce your speaker's name, but look at the speaker and smile. Make it apparent that you are genuinely happy to receive the speaker, then quietly return to your seat.

The following sample speech is a good example of an effective introduction of a speaker:

> Members of the City Council and distinguished guests: it is my privilege to introduce to you today the police commissioner, who will address us on the subject of measures to counteract crime in our community. Most of you know that the commissioner has a distinguished record as head of our police force for more than ten years. However, you may not know that he also holds a doctorate in criminology and studied abroad for a year with Interpol—the international police force.
>
> One of the commissioner's favorite projects has been the Neighborhood Watch Program—in which citizens are encouraged to keep an eye on their neighbors' houses and report any suspicious activity to the police. When the commissioner first proposed this idea, he was accused of "reinventing the busybody." The Morning Herald ran an editorial headlined "First Busybody of the City," in which it pictured townspeople lurking behind their curtains and jotting down the license plate numbers of their neighbors' relatives.
>
> Well, the "First Busybody" has gotten the last laugh. Since the program was inaugurated a year ago, burglaries

and vandalism in parts of our city have decreased by 30 percent! Today the commissioner is going to tell us more about
how the program works and how it can be expanded to other
areas of the community. I am sure we will all be interested to
hear what he has to say. Please welcome Police Commissioner Patrick McCarter.[1]

CHAPTER **20**

PRESENTING A GIFT
OR AWARD

IF YOU are called upon to take part in a presentation ceremony, your task will be to relate in an interesting, informative, cordial, and inspiring way the reasons the recipient is
receiving the gift or award. Perhaps the recipient is being
honored for long service, for excelling in performance, for
winning a competition, or for changing status, as in getting
married or moving to another city.

The speech of presentation on such an occasion should be
relatively brief. It may be no more than the simple announcement: "And the winner is...." Or, it may be up to
four or five minutes, depending upon the audience and the
occasion.

In making your presentation you should include the following information:

• State who is giving the gift or award, unless this information is already evident.

• State the reason the gift or award is being presented, and
what it represents.

• Tell the audience why the recipient was selected, point-
ing out the achievements, contributions, or situation of the
recipient. Concentrate on the specific contributions and

achievements that relate to the award, not on other aspects of the recipient's life.

• Remember that as presenter you will be speaking not for yourself only, but for all of those gathered to honor the recipient. Try to express appropriately their esteem or admiration, as well as your own.

• If the award was won in a public competition, acknowledge the other competitors as well, and commend their efforts also.

• Make an inspiring, effective closing to your speech, and then give the recipient the gift or award, if this act is included in your responsibilities.

The following example of a speech of presentation was delivered by Gregory Peck when presenting the Jean Hersholt Humanitarian Award to Danny Kaye at the 1982 Academy Awards ceremony:

It's a long trip from Brooklyn to Buckingham Palace, and it's a far piece from Beverly Hills to an obscure village in Bangladesh. Danny Kaye has made both journeys, sustained by his remarkable gifts, his grace, and his intelligence. He has been a star of the first magnitude since his remarkable talent exploded on the Broadway stage in *Lady in the Dark* in 1941, and one who has had a high sense of priority: his wife, Sylvia, and daughter, Dena, have always come first in his life—and then, in no special order, his work, the world's children and great music.

For UNICEF (United Nations International Children's Emergency Fund), he continues to travel the world, bringing joy and hope to children on all the continents, and initiating programs to save them from hunger and give them a better chance in life. He has been doing this for years, with no pay and without fanfare. No trumpets. No headlines. His reward, the laughter of children.

As forbearing and skillful as he is with children, so he is

with symphony orchestras, groups of seventy or eighty highly disciplined artists. He cannot read music, yet he has conducted major orchestras all over the world with musicianship that is sensitive, completely serious, and, at times, likely to veer off alarmingly into the hilarious. Danny's irrepressible *joie de vivre* makes his concerts joyous occasions for musicians and audiences alike. Bach and Mozart have no better friend. Nor have the orchestras and their pension funds. Nor have we.

And thus, for his prodigious labors for the children of the world, for the wondrous people who make music, the Board of Governors proudly gives the Jean Hersholt Humanitarian Award to a "Citizen of the World" who does honor to our profession—Mr. Danny Kaye.[1]

CHAPTER 21

ACCEPTING A GIFT
OR AWARD

IF YOU are the recipient of a gift or award, your acceptance remarks should be brief, humble, appreciative, and gracious.

Consider the following suggestions as you prepare acceptance:

- Express appreciation for the gift and award.
- Express gratitude to the givers for their generosity and kindness in bestowing it upon you.
- State that you are honored and pleased because you have always had a respect for and a fondness of the group bestowing the honor.
- If you were selected from a group of outstanding competitors or teammates, express your respect for and appreciation of their abilities and skills and your belief that several of them were as deserving of the award as you.
- If appropriate, express appreciation to the people who helped you gain the award through their advice or instruction. Be specific.
- State what the gift or award means to you in inspiring you to greater service or accomplishments.

The following speech was delivered by Dr. Martin Luther King, Jr. in 1964 when he accepted the Nobel Peace Prize. It is a good example of a gracious acceptance speech.

You honor the ground crew without whose labor and sacrifice the jetlights to freedom could never have left the earth.

Most of these people will never make the headlines and their names will not appear in Who's Who. Yet the years have rolled past and when the blazing light of truth is focused on this marvelous age in which we live—men and women will know and children will be taught that we have a finer land, a better people, a more noble civilization—because these humble children of God were willing to suffer for righteousness' sake.

I think Alfred Nobel would know what I mean when I say that I accept this award in the spirit of a curator of some precious heirloom which he holds in trust for its true owners— all those to whom beauty is truth and truth beauty—and in whose eyes the beauty of genuine brotherhood and peace is more precious than diamonds or silver or gold.[1]

CHAPTER 22

DELIVERING A EULOGY

IF YOU are asked to deliver a eulogy at a funeral or at a commemorative occasion, your responsibility will be to give your audience a greater appreciation of, and admiration for, the life and accomplishments of the person you are honoring. Your primary goal will be to evoke emotion, to make the person live again in the minds of the listeners, to generate respect for the person, and to draw inspiration from the person's best qualities and character.

In composing your eulogy you should select some outstanding aspects of the person's life or services as a basis for your comments. You can build the eulogy around the qualities that made the person great: the major purpose of the person's life, the lessons we may learn from the person, the inspiration we can draw from the person's life.

Perhaps you can build your speech upon an appropriate quotation that summarizes the person's life and shows how the person manifested the admirable traits described in the quotation. (See the last section of this manual for selected quotations.) You may want to use a verse from a biblical source or other religious reference that is particularly apt, or perhaps an historic figure with whom you can favorably compare the deceased.

You can use one or more of these themes and develop

them by using illustrations, by telling of incidents that illustrate a basic character trait, by relating conversations, or by showing how the person's work benefited society.

In composing your eulogy, try to be creative in your use of language. Select language that will be impressive and inspiring, that paints pictures. Try to use language that will lend dignity and meaning to the occasion and that will evoke honest emotion.

CHAPTER 23

COMMENCEMENT ADDRESS

DELIVERING A commencement address offers a challenge to even the most qualified public speaker. Too many young graduates momentarily lose their zeal for the occasion as they are lulled into passivity by a droning voice. They are frequently told they are "standing at the crossroad of life" and that the future belongs to them. How does a speaker say something new for an occasion steeped in traditional rhetoric?

Begin by selecting a theme that you can develop through specific illustrations and personal insight. While themes for a commencement exercise are subject to great variety, a top priority in selecting your theme is to focus upon the interests, issues, dreams, and ambitions of the graduating class. While your audience may include many a crying babe and proud grandparent, you are talking primarily to the graduating class and should give their interests due consideration. Perhaps you've been away from "the school scene" for quite some time and are unsure about the topics that interest contemporary youth. Call the school and ask to arrange a conversation with a representative of the graduating class—perhaps the president or the editor of the newspaper or annual.

Most commencement speakers select a somewhat serious

theme for their speech although a light theme can include provocative ideas. However, unless you have achieved the fame of Bob Hope or Carol Burnett, avoid too much levity and stick to a few entertaining quips or anecdotes. Making your address specific to the school will personalize your speech for the audience. Perhaps you are an alumnus or alumnae of the school and can recall a special incident or faculty member. Perhaps you have been an avid follower of the school's sports team, magazine sales record, or academic record. The personal illustrations will enliven your speech, and the audience will feel increased pride in their school.

Whether your theme is serious or light-hearted, avoid becoming enmeshed in an emotional oration. Since the occasion is in itself emotional, the speaker needs to maintain a sense of dignity and control. Of course, you can touch on an emotional point or two in your speech, but then move on toward the conclusion.

Other guidelines for a commencement address include:

1. *Limit your speech* to a maximum of twenty minutes. A twelve to fifteen minute speech would probably win even more approval from the audience and would be appreciated by those parents with the crying babies.

2. *Congratulate the graduating class.* For many of the students, commencement marks the culmination of many years of hard work and long-term commitment. They deserve a well-stated congratulations.

3. *Maintain a positive outlook* in your speech. Commencement exercises are not the time to embark on a platform against nuclear holocaust or the rape of the environment. The occasion is a happy one for most students and should be treated as such.

4. *Speak as loudly and clearly as necessary* to reach the outer boundaries of your audience. Because the audience is

usually a large one, you need to make an extra effort to insure your voice is being heard.

5. *Attempt to inspire* your audience. While the graduating class may be far younger in years, do not underestimate their need to hear creative and enduring insights into life—not dull, didactic statements about how to succeed by "keeping their noses to the grindstone."

6. *Use interesting quotations* that are neither too complex to absorb on one hearing nor too simplistic. In fact, a single quotation can serve as a springboard for the development of your entire speech.

7. *Prepare diligently* to organize your thoughts. Use carefully selected ideas, illustrations, and words, and your speech will be met by an approving audience.

CHAPTER 24

INSPIRATIONAL SPEECH

AN INSPIRATIONAL speech (also called a motivational or persuasive speech) should be one that stimulates the listeners, either by motivating them to action or encouraging them to consider a new idea. This type of speech, much needed and usually appreciated, inspires a sense of hope, courage, and vision in the listener.

Before a sports event or performance of a play, an inspirational speech can make the difference between mediocrity and a great performance. Anytime people need encouragement to give their best effort, an inspirational speech is appropriate.

Success in delivering such a speech depends largely on how imaginative you are in your writing. Above all, however, the success depends upon how skillful you are in your delivery.

Outstanding persuasive speeches have been written by Daniel Webster, Abraham Lincoln, and Franklin D. Roosevelt. Each of the following characterized their successful speeches:

a. Contained emotional content
b. Suggested new options
c. Capitalized on their individuality

A motivational speech must be tightly organized with no flabbiness of content. To evoke a response from the audience every point must be succinct and forceful.

CHAPTER 25

SPEECH OF WELCOME

THE PURPOSE of a formal speech of welcome at a public gathering is to acknowledge the presence of an individual or group and to extend a warm greeting. The speaker may make the speech from a personal standpoint, but in most cases is a representative of the entire audience. Occasions requiring this type of speech include conventions, religious gatherings, seminars, memorial celebrations, initiations, and high school and college reunions.

A speech of welcome should be brief but sincere. It should touch on the reason for the welcome, the importance of the occasion, and the expectation that the audience will benefit greatly from the association with those being welcomed.

One occasion for this type of speech is to welcome new citizens after they have taken the oath of allegiance. Keep your remarks simple and easy to comprehend. You may need to slow the pace of your speech to ensure that those for whom English is not a primary language are following your remarks.

You may want to have the speech printed in bulletin form or on a card so that the guests may have a keepsake of the event. If all of the guests are from other countries, you may wish to open your speech with a welcoming sentence in several different languages.

In the event that you are welcoming the return of a "Favorite Son" for a particular community, keep your remarks centered on the honoree. Recollections of humorous events of the past and noting praiseworthy events in the honoree's life are generally included in this type of speech. Keep your remarks brief and upbeat; avoid being solicitous or overshadowed by the accomplishments of the honoree.

Other suggestions for a speech of welcome include:

1. Addressing the guest by name at the outset of your speech. This technique reinforces the name for the audience and personalizes your message to the guest.

2. If you are welcoming foreign visitors or new citizens, do not inform them about how fortunate they are to be on U.S. territory. The visitors or new citizens are probably aware of the attributes of this country. Instead, invite them to explore the town (city or state) and wish them well in their adventures.

3. Express your reasons for the welcome. For example, if you are welcoming new members into a club, tell them you look forward to working with them and look forward to getting to know them.

4. Describe the mutual benefit you and the visitor, new citizen, or new club member will receive from your interaction.

5. Avoid embarrassing your guest with too much praise or needless exaggerations. Do not expect a response from the recipient of your welcome unless this has been prearranged.

The following speech of welcome given by Carol Larson at an initiation banquet of Kappa Kappa Gamma Sorority on Founder's Day, October 1951, at San José State College conveys in an imaginative way the warmth with which the group of initiates are received by members of the sorority.

Address of Welcome
By Carol Larson

This reminds me so much of a family reunion of very great distinction—there are very few families who can say that eighty-one years ago they started out with six and now have over 40,000 sisters!

But now, think back, if you will, to your pledge-training days. Remember how everything seemed so mysterious and exciting? It was just as if Kappa had given you a bright-colored treasure box full of, oh so many things. As you examined each object you marveled at its value and beauty. Of course, there were some things you didn't understand, but our Kappa sisters were more than willing to help you.

You uncovered information on almost every phase of Kappa, but just think of all the intangible and invaluable treasures you found—lifelong friendships and loyalties, graciousness, confidence, understanding.

Then, as the weeks passed by you noticed that the box was getting emptier and as you surveyed all the fine things, you might have felt a little sorry that it was coming to an end.

Then you discovered a little compartment in the box that could only be opened by a tiny, exquisite, golden key. And you new initiates, because Kappa felt that you were ready to wear the golden key and accept with it all the privileges and challenges that follow, you were allowed to open up that compartment. At first glance at the untold treasures you'd never even dreamed of, you probably thought, "Why, I've only skimmed the surface, the best is yet to come!"

Yes, you have much to look forward to. One thing you're going to discover is that no matter how much you gain from Kappa there always seems to be so much more. And the more you give, the more you get! And, as the years go by, you're going to add little treasures of your own to Kappa so that others may find and appreciate them. There are many Sisters here tonight who have been never-ending contributors, and each time they do contribute, their lives grow more beautiful and happier!

As newly initiated Kappas you are beginning one of the most wonderful experiences you could ever hope to have. May your lives be full of the treasures of Kappa Kappa Gamma, and may you share them as they come to you. We're all so very proud to welcome you as Sisters!

CHAPTER 26

RESPONSE TO
SPEECH OF WELCOME

SOME SPEECHES of welcome require a response from the
person or spokesperson for the group being welcomed. Such
a response should include a simple "thank you" to the person who offered the welcoming remarks and to the group. A
response to a speech of welcome may be required when a
person visits a foreign country and is presented to a particular organization or club, when a person is a special guest at
a meeting or conference, or as the introduction of a keynote
address or other occasional speech.

The following abbreviated sample may be a helpful guide-
line for constructing your response:

> Thank you (person's name and group's name). I appreci-
> ate the words of welcome, and I wish to thank you on behalf
> of (group represented) for the warmth of your greeting. We
> are delighted to be here for several reasons. (State specific
> reasons). We are looking forward to sharing with you (bene-
> fits of the event). You have offered warm hospitality, and we
> appreciate your graciousness. Thank you.

Anticipate the occasion when you may need a response to
a welcome. A few well-selected words will further enhance
your role as honored guest.

CHAPTER 27

SPEECHES FOR PATRIOTIC OCCASIONS

CEREMONIES IN observance of national holidays and other patriotic occasions such as political and civic gatherings are frequently times of speechmaking. If you are asked to speak on a patriotic occasion, assume that some measure of flag-waving and sentiment is in order. Of course, you must tailor your speech to fit the occasion, but the underlying theme should be one of unabashed patriotism and pride in our national heritage.

Unfortunately, patriotic speeches are among the dullest; it seems many of these speeches begin with the premise that the past is dead and their speeches do nothing to bring it alive. Instead, as you write a speech with a patriotic theme, strive to present old themes and ideas in new and interesting ways.

On what occasions would someone be asked to deliver a patriotic speech? Independence Day, Memorial Day, and Veterans Day are perhaps the most common, but a president's birthday, Martin Luther King Day, Armed Forces Day, and United Nations Day (to name a few) are all commemorations for which a patriotic speech would be in order.

Some tips for writing a patriotic speech are as follows:

1. *Include brief quotations, poems, and interesting references* to historical figures. Avoid the overstated facts that everyone has known since elementary school days. Use poems that are comprehensible within reason; you will lose your audience with an abstract poem that perhaps requires several readings and some mulling over to grasp its meaning.

2. *Read reliable biographies or well-written histories* to learn some new information about a historical figure or event. Present a new insight so that your audience has the opportunity to learn something new.

3. *Remember that the content of your speech is inseparable from you* as presenter. Some patriotic speeches are most effective when presented by a bold or dramatic speaker. Mold your speech so it fits your personal style. Remember that Abraham Lincoln, Elizabeth Cady Stanton, and Franklin D. Roosevelt all had important ideas to present to an audience, but each had a unique style reflecting the individual's personality.

4. *Help your audience claim its heritage and celebrate the occasion* with pride. You can inspire strong sentiments by reminding your audience of the past if you give them a fresh perspective from which to view it.

The following selections have patriotic themes. You may want to quote portions of these excerpts as you prepare your speech.

Washington's Prayer for the Nation

Written at Newburg, June 8, 1783, and sent to the governors of all the States.

Almighty God, we make our earnest prayer that Thou wilt keep the United States in Thy holy protection, that Thou wilt incline the hearts of the citizens to cultivate a spirit of subordination and obedience to government, and entertain a brotherly affection and love for one another and for their citizens of the United States at large.

And finally that Thou wilt most graciously be pleased to dispose us all to do justice, to love mercy, and to demean ourselves with that charity, humility, and pacific temper of mind which were the characteristics of the Divine Author of our blessed religion, and without an humble imitation of whose example in these things, we can never hope to be a happy nation.

Grant our supplications, we beseech Thee, through Jesus Christ our Lord. Amen.

Abraham Lincoln

From an address delivered at the Auditorium, Chicago, February 12, 1895 by Henry L. Watterson.

Throughout the wild contention that preceded the war, amid the lurid passions that attended the war itself, not one bitter or narrow word escaped the lips of Abraham Lincoln, whilst there was hardly a day that he was not projecting his big, sturdy personality between some Southern man or woman and danger.

From Caesar to Bismarck and Gladstone, the world has had its statesmen and its soldiers-men who rose to eminence and power step by step, through a series of geometric progression, as it were, each advancement following in regular order one after the other, the whole obedient to well-established and well-understood laws of cause and effect. They were not what we call "men of destiny." They were "men of the time." They were men whose careers had a beginning, a middle, and an end, rounding of lives with histories, full, it may be, of interesting and exciting events, but comprehensive and comprehensible; simple, clear complete.

The inspired men are fewer. Whence their emanation, where and how they got their power, and by what rule they lived, moved, and had their being, we know not. There is no explication to their lives. They rose from shadow and they went in mist. We see them, feel them, but we know them not. They came, God's word upon their lips; they did their office, God's mantle about them; and they passed away, God's holy light between the world and them, leaving behind a memory, half mortal and half myth. From first to last they were the creations of some special Providence, baffling the wit of man to fathom, defeating the machinations of the world, the flesh, and the devil, and their work done, passing from the scene as mysteriously as they had come upon it.

Tried by this standard, where shall we find an illustration more impressive than—Abraham Lincoln, whose career might be chanted by a Greek chorus as at once the prelude and the epilogue of the most imperial theme of modern times.

Born as lowly as the Son of God, in a hovel; of what ancestry we know not and care not; reared in penury, squalor, with no gleam of light or fair surroundings; without external graces, actual or acquired; without name or fame of official training; it was reserved for this strange being, late in life, to be snatched from obscurity, raised to supreme command at a supreme moment, and intrusted with the destiny of a nation.

The great leaders of his party, the most experienced and accomplished public men of the day, were made to stand aside; were sent to the rear, whilst this fantastic figure was led by unseen hands to the front and given the reins of power. It is immaterial whether we were for him or against him—wholly immaterial. That, during four years, carrying with them such a pressure of responsibility as the world never witnessed before, he filled the vast space allotted him in the eyes and actions of mankind, is to say that he was inspired of God, for nowhere else could he have acquired the wisdom and the grace indispensable to his mission.

Where did Shakespeare get his genius? Where did Mozart get his music? Whose hand smote the lyre of the Scottish plowman, and stayed the life of the German priest? God, God, and God alone; and as surely as these were raised up by God, inspired by God, was Abraham Lincoln; and a thousand years hence, no story, no tragedy, no epic poem will be filled with greater wonder, or be followed by mankind with deeper feeling, than that which tells of his life and death.

The Gettysburg Address

November 19, 1863

Four score and seven years ago our fathers brought forth on this continent, a new nation, conceived in Liberty, and dedicated to the proposition that all men are created equal.

Now we are engaged in a great civil war, testing whether that nation or any nation so conceived and so dedicated, can long endure. We are met on a great battle-field of that war. We have come to dedicate a portion of that field, as a final resting place for those who here gave their lives that that nation might live. It is altogether fitting and proper that we should do this.

But, in a larger sense, we can not dedicate—we can not consecrate—we can not hallow—this ground. The brave men, living and dead, who struggled here, have consecrated it, far above our poor power to add or detract. The world will little note, nor long remember what we say here, but it can never forget what they did here. It is for us the living, rather, to be dedicated here to the unfinished work which they who fought here thus far so nobly advanced. It is rather for us to be here dedicated to the great task remaining before us—that from these honored dead we take increased devotion to that cause for which they gave the last full measure of devotion—that we here highly resolve that these dead shall not have died in vain—that this nation, under God, shall have a new birth of freedom—and that government of the people, by the people, for the people, shall not perish from the earth.

FLAG

The Flag-raising on Iwo Jima

(This CBS broadcast was given by Don Pryor, correspondent, from the flying bridge of Admiral Turner's amphibious flagship off the coast of Iwo Jima on February 23, 1945, when the United States Marines raised the American flag on Mount Suribachi on Iwo Jima, the Japanese Gibraltar of the Pacific.)

This afternoon over Iwo Jima you could see the most beautiful sight in the world—the Stars and Stripes fluttering, small but triumphant, high on the topmost ridge of the Suribachi volcano.

Four other correspondents, a couple of Marines and I, watched a small group of the 28th Marines winding their way painfully up towards the crest this morning, as we waited on the beach for a boat to bring us out here to the flagship. They had fought their way against opposition, up sheer rock cliffs on ladders. And on, and on, and on up the steep rocky sides of the upper slopes, while the Japs threw hand grenades from above, peppered them with rifle and machine-gun fire.

I understand that the flagpole is a steel rod carried in sections which each man added to his already heavy burden. I didn't hear that they had made it until we were back aboard the flagship. A sophisticated correspondent came into the wardroom shouting, 'They've raised Old Glory on the top of Suribachi!' Old Glory! We all rushed to the portholes to see. And there, sure enough, it was—tiny and wonderful, standing clear against the sky above that awful mountain. Nobody talked about it much.

The Message of the Flag

It speaks to me, this wondrous weave
Of red and white and blue;

God grant my list'ning heart receive
And hold its message true!
A symbol mere—to me it seems
By rarest life endowed,
As in the radiant sun it gleams,
Or flaunts the sullen cloud.

It speaks in every crimson line
Of blood for freedom shed;
It tells of glorious deeds divine,
Of hallowed martyred dead.
In humble bed they lie;
And yet they live again,
To speak, to strive, to fight, to die,
For love of fellow men.

Lo, from the white, in accents pure,
Untinged by selfishness
The words of sages, strong and sure,
The crimson stains caress;
Those words which, through countless years,
Have hero hearts sustained,
Have swept away the mists of tears,
And marked the freedom gained.

And from the vaulted sky above,
The stars eternal sign
The matchless, boundless, holy love,
Of him, our Heav'nly King!
Lo, from the blue the voice declares
The triumph of the good;
Each star in equal honor shares
The common brotherhood.

Float on, O Flag! Thy mystic thought
With love my soul inspires!
Thy voice, by loyal heart strings caught,
Seems turned to heav'nly choirs!
I answer thee! I promise thee
My life, my love, my all!
Float on! Float on! For Liberty!
I'll hear, if thou dost call!
        –Author unknown

Memorial Day Address

This speech, by Oliver Wendell Holmes, was delivered on May 30, 1884 in Keene, New Hampshire to the John Sedgwick Post No. 4, Grand Army of the Republic.

Not long ago I heard a young man ask why people still kept up Memorial Day, and it set me thinking of the answer. Not the answer that you and I should give to each other— not the expression of those feelings that, so long as you and I live, will make this day sacred to memories of love and grief and heroic youth—but an answer which should command the assent of those who do not share our memories, and in which we of the North and our brethren of the South could join in perfect accord...

The soldiers of the war need no explanations: they can join in commemorating a soldier's death with feelings not different in kind, whether he fell toward them or by their side.

But Memorial Day may and ought to have a meaning also for those who do not share our memories. When men have instinctively agreed to celebrate an anniversary, it will be found that there is some thought or feeling behind it which is too large to be dependent upon associations alone. The Fourth of July, for instance, has still its serious aspect, although we no longer should think of rejoicing like children that we have escaped from an outgrown control, although we have achieved not only our national but our moral independence and know it far too profoundly to make a talk about it, and although an Englishman can join the celebration without a scruple. For, stripped of the temporary associations which gave rise to it, it is now the moment when by common consent we pause to become conscious of our national life and to rejoice in it, to recall what our country has done for each of us, and to ask ourselves what we can do for our country in return.

So to the indifferent inquirer who asks why Memorial Day is still kept we may answer: it celebrates and solemnly reaffirms from year to year a national act of enthusiasm and faith. It embodies in the most impressive form our belief that to act with enthusiasm and faith is the condition of acting greatly. To fight out a war, you must believe something and want something with all your might. So must you do to carry anything else to an end worth reaching. More than that, you must be willing to commit yourself to a course, perhaps a long and hard one, without being able to foresee exactly where you will come out. All that is required of you is that you should go somewhither as hard as ever you can. The rest belongs to fate. One may fall—at the beginning of the charge or at the top of the earthworks, but in no other way can he reach the rewards of victory.

When it was felt so deeply as it was on both sides that a man ought to take part in the war unless some conscientious scruple or strong practical reason made it impossible, was that feeling simply the requirement of a local majority that their neighbors should agree with them? I think not: I think the feeling was right,—in the South as in the North. I think that, as life is action and passion, it is required of a man that he should share the passion and action of his time at peril of being judged not to have lived.

If this be so, the use of this day is obvious. It is true that I cannot argue a man into a desire. If he says to me, Why should I wish to know the secrets of philosophy? Why see to decipher the hidden laws of creation that are graven upon the tablets of the rocks, or to unravel the history of civilization that is woven in the tissue of our jurisprudence, or to do any great work, either of speculation or of practical affairs? I cannot answer him: or at least my answer is as little worth making for any effect it will have upon his wishes as if he asked why should I eat this, or drink that. You must begin by wanting to. But although desire cannot be imparted by argument, it can be by contagion. Feeling begets feeling, and great feeling begets great feeling. We can hardly share the emotions that make this day to us the most sacred day of the year, and embody them in ceremonial pomp, without in some degree imparting them to those who come after us. I believe from the bottom of my heart that our memorial halls and statues and tablets, the tattered flags of our regiments gathered in the State houses, and this day with its funeral march and decorated graves, are worth more to our young men by way of chastening and inspiration than the monuments of another hundred years of peaceful life could be.

But even if I am wrong, even if those who come after us are to forget all that we hold dear, and the future is to teach and kindle its children in ways as yet unrevealed, it is enough for us that to us this day is dear and sacred...

CHAPTER 28

SPEECH OF TRIBUTE

A SPEECH of tribute is given in honor of someone for an outstanding achievement or exemplary contribution. This type of speech usually occurs at a testimonial dinner, a retirement ceremony, a political gathering, or any other occasion when a person is saluted. Building a greater appreciation of the honoree and offering thanks for his or her contribution are two major elements of a speech of tribute.

The tribute may be as brief as several sentences or a full, fifteen-to-twenty minute oration. However, a detailed biography from the earliest years of childhood or a long list of accomplishments is of little interest except to a doting family member.

If your speech is to be a full-scale one, include information and ideas that reach beyond biographical data and challenge your audience to effect change in their own lives. Shift the focus away from the honoree at times and relate characteristics embodied by the honoree to the audience.

Humorous recollections that can be shared with the audience are particularly helpful to enliven this type of speech. They serve to remind the audience that the honoree is, in fact, a member of the human race with shortcomings and eccentricities. However, remember that one of your primary purposes is to cite the valuable contributions made by the honoree; he or she has done something exceptional and certainly merits the tribute.

To learn more about the life of the honoree, interview family members, friends, and co-workers. Question them about many facets of the honoree's life, although avoid being too personal or prying. If the honoree has been featured in newspapers, magazines, or books, review these sources so you have a thorough biographical picture. While not wanting to embarrass the honoree, try to find fresh information— a story or anecdote that few people in the audience have heard.

Audiovisuals can be particularly effective in depicting the valuable deeds of the honoree. Also, these aids provide an opportunity to inject humor into what often becomes a dull monologue.

CHAPTER 29

SPEECH OF DEDICATION

A SPEECH at the dedication of a new business, building, or institution is essentially a speech of celebration. Your responsibility is to express happiness for the completion of the initial stages of operation, perhaps to trace the formative stages of the project, and to offer hope for the success of further endeavors.

As you inform the audience of the developmental stages of the project, be wary of boring your listeners with irrelevant detail or cumbersome statistics. If the building being dedicated is named to honor a person, describe some of the outstanding qualities of this person's life which merited this honor. Again, avoid a full-scale biography and dwell only on that which relates to this public occasion.

A dedication speech is generally incorporated into a formal ceremony, and the speech should reflect the mood of the occasion. While some speakers exploit the occasion as an opportunity to wax eloquent with high-flung phrases, beware of losing your audience in unneccessary wordiness.

One approach to the dedicatory speech is to focus upon a special architectural feature of the building. A beautifully designed entrance or window can serve as a basis for a few words about new beginnings or a "greater vision," which is enhanced by the new building.

If your speech is to be written for the dedication of a government building, approach your topic with caution. Some people are not pleased at the idea of expanded government facilities. This type of speech would probably be better received in a small-town situation as opposed to another Washington office.

Your responsibility is to be creative in your choice of language in order to elevate your listeners' regard for the occasion. Express sentiments that convey warmth and set a positive mood of celebration.

CHAPTER **30**

AFTER-DINNER SPEECH

AN AFTER-DINNER speech is generally construed as entertainment for the audience. The setting is usually relaxed, as the audience finishes the final bites of chocolate mousse or cherry tart and sits back to listen. Unlike the keynote address, which is nearly always built around a serious topic, the after-dinner speech can delight the audience with anecdotes and yarns woven together with a unifying theme.

If you have an assigned topic or have chosen a serious theme, advanced preparation for the audience will help mold their expectations. Including the speech's title in a program or newsletter can do much to ensure the audience's expectations are not dashed by a twenty-minute speech on wildflowers in Argentina when all along they expected a five-minute travelogue of your southern trek.

If you will be introduced by a toastmaster, you may want to have some heavy verbal artillery ready to combat a humorous assault. Toastmasters are often masters of the finely tuned phrase, and a ready response could come in handy. However, don't feel you must be witty at the expense of losing dignity; if repartee is not your gift, a polite response or "thank you" is quite satisfactory.

Because of the relaxed atmosphere, make every effort not to read your speech. Your rapport with the audience will be much stronger if you can engage them through a relaxed manner and eye contact.

If you do want to include amusing material in your speech, where do you go for sources?

1. Consider your local library for references on speech-making.

2. Recall incidents and anecdotes from your own life.

3. Relate a scene from a current movie, radio, or television program (just don't give away the ending).

4. Reflect upon an unusual person you've known, perhaps an eccentric aunt or the person down the street whose window you shattered years ago in a neighborhood ball game.

5. Tell a good joke. This attempt at entertainment must be approached only by those who have a sixth sense for what is an affront to no one.

6. Visual aids may also add interest to an after-dinner speech. Limit their use to approximately five minutes so that they do not overshadow your speech. (If your sole purpose is to do a visual presentation, then that is another subject.) If you show slides, edit them carefully so only the most pertinent are included. You do not want to turn the lights on to find that you've lost your entire audience to an after-dinner snooze. Furthermore, be sure you are entirely comfortable with the A-V equipment—whether it's slides, a videotape machine, or a 35 mm projector. If you need to arrange assistance beforehand, do so in order to prevent embarrassing lulls as you fumble for switches and cords.

An after-dinner speech is frequently fifteen or twenty minutes, though the occasion dictates the length of time. If you are the featured speaker, your speech should be more fully developed than if you are one of several speakers. Before you begin speech preparation, ask the host for time guidelines.

Often an after-dinner speech will end with a toast or tribute to an honored person. Be prepared, if a tribute or toast is on the agenda, to have your remarks include a reference from your speech to reinforce your topic and relate it to the honoree.

CHAPTER **31**

SPEECH FOR HIGH SCHOOL OR COLLEGE REUNIONS

IF YOU are the featured speaker at a high school or college reunion, remember that you speak not only for yourself, but for the entire group assembled. The most popular speaker for this occasion will be one who is brief and entertaining; a long oration is neither expected nor desired.

A reunion is a time of nostalgia, of looking back. Be sure to include in your speech cherished school memories that will be remembered by everyone—not just a few. You may want to mention the school building, athletic events with their triumphs and defeats, the cheering in the stands, the excitement of the band. You can reflect on times of learning and times of merrymaking and recall the joyous occasion after all the months and years of tedious preparation. A few words of appreciation to the faculty that served you and to the community for their support are always appropriate.

Waxing sentimental is no longer acceptable when few students have the close ties to schools that were once commonplace. A transient culture and varied levels of school (elementary, junior high, high school) make remote the days of twelve years in one school or four years in one college. The days of "ivy covered walls" and "hallowed halls" are not as prevalent. Therefore, it is important that your speech ring true to the students' experience in a particular school. Recalling peculiar fads in clothing, music, and entertainment can stir some collective memories in your former classmates.

You can also express what the school meant to you while you were there and take note of any lasting values that have sustained you since graduation. Bring to light any outstanding successes that have been achieved by graduates of your class. Pause for a moment of silence in memory of any classmates who have died.

To bring the focus from the past to the present, express thanks for the opportunity to re-establish friendships and look forward to meeting again. If you know the date of the next class reunion, announce it, urge those present to return and share "new" memories, and encourage classmates to keep in touch with one another in the intervening time.

CHAPTER 32

TOASTS—WEDDING, RETIREMENT, AND TESTIMONIAL

A TOAST is an expression of good wishes or appreciation for the honoree. There are any number of occasions on which it is appropriate to propose a toast: an engagement party, a wedding rehearsal dinner, a wedding reception, a wedding anniversary, a retirement dinner, a testimonial dinner. All of these occasions are cause for celebration. The purpose of a wedding toast is to express hope for the future happiness and well-being of the wedding couple. The purpose of a toast at a retirement dinner or testimonial dinner is to express appreciation for the service and accomplishments of the honoree.

You will appear more poised and confident if you have time to prepare an appropriate toast, but if you are asked unexpectedly to propose a toast and have not had time to plan what you would like to say, you can simply say what you feel. A toast can be as simple as "To John, a wonderful friend and associate," or "To Bill, whose life has been an inspiration to me."

If you do have advance warning, you can include a few appropriate remarks of remembrance or praise, tell a relevant story, or interject a little humor.

The following sample toasts will be helpful to you in preparing your toasts:

A Father's Toast at His Daughter's Engagement Party

1. Now you know that the reason for this party is to announce Mary's engagement to John. I would like to propose a toast to them both, wishing them many years of happiness in their life together.

2. Mary's mother and I have always looked forward to meeting the man Mary would choose to marry. We knew she'd pick a winner, but we never dared hope he'd be as fine a person as John. We want you all to know how pleased we are to announce their engagement tonight. Please join me in wishing them a long and happy marriage.

A Best Man's Toast at the Rehearsal Dinner

1. For some time I have been worried about Mary and John's apparent incompatibility, but looking at them tonight I see how wrong I have been. So, please join me in a toast to John's income and Mary's patibility.

2. John and I have been friends for a long time now, and I have always known what a lucky guy he is. Tonight all of you can see what I mean when you look at Mary and realize she is to become his bride tomorrow. Please join me in a toast to Mary and John. May this kind of luck continue throughout their lives together.

A Best Man's Toast to the Bridal Couple at the Wedding Reception

1. To Mary and John—a beautiful girl, a wonderful man—and the happiest couple I ever hope to see!

2. To Mary and John—may they always be as happy as they look today.

A Bridegroom's Toast to His Bride at the Wedding Reception

1. I'd like you all to join me in a toast to the girl who's just

made me the happiest man in the world.

2. All my life I've wondered what the girl I'd marry would be like. In my wildest dreams I never imagined she would be as wonderful as Mary, so please join me in drinking this first toast to my bride.

A Bridegroom's Father's Toast at the Rehearsal Dinner

1. I would like to ask you to join me in drinking a toast to two wonderful people without whom this wedding could never have been possible: Mary's mother and father, Mr. and Mrs. Brown.

2. I don't need to tell you what a wonderful girl Mary is, but I do want to tell you how happy John's mother and I are to welcome her as our new daughter-in-law. To Mary and John.

Toast to a Retiring Employee or a Member of the Firm

1. It is often said that nobody is indispensable, and that may sometimes be true, but for all of us there will never be anyone who can replace Joe. Although we will miss him greatly, we know how much he is looking forward to his retirement and we wish him all the happiness he so richly deserves in the years to come.

2. I know that everyone of us here tonight thinks of Bob (Mr. Smith) not as an employee (employer) but as a friend. When he leaves, we will suffer a very real loss both in our organization and in our hearts. At the same time we rejoice that he will now be able to enjoy the things he wants to do, so let us rise and drink a toast to one of the finest friends we have known.

Anniversary Toast

1. Many of us who are here tonight can well remember that day twenty-five years ago when we drank a toast to the future happiness of Mary and Bob. It is more than obvious that our good wishes at that time have served them well, and therefore I would like to ask that all of you—old friends and

new—rise and drink with me to another twenty-five years of the same love and happiness that Mary and Bob have already shared together.

2. John, I'd like to propose a toast to you on your fiftieth birthday. It has been a wonderful party tonight and all of us wish you health, wealth, and the years to enjoy them.

Toast to a Guest of Honor at a Testimonial Dinner

1. We are gathered here tonight to honor a man who has given unselfishly of his time and effort to make this campaign so successful. Without the enthusiasm and leadership that Bob Jones has shown all through these past months, we could never have reached our goal. Please join me in drinking a toast to the man who more than anyone else is responsible for making it possible to see our dream of a new hospital wing finally come true.

2. Ladies and gentlemen, you have already heard of the magnificent work our guest of honor has accomplished during his past two years in Washington. Right now we would like to tell him that no matter how proud we are of his success in his chosen career, we are even more pleased to have him home with us again. It's great to have you back, Jim![1]

CHAPTER **33**

MAKING ANNOUNCEMENTS

IN ALMOST any type of meeting there will be a need for announcements. Such announcements usually are best placed at the close of the meeting, just before adjournment. However, an announcement may be needed in connection with some order of business at any time during the course of a meeting.

If you are designated to make an announcement, there are certain essentials that you need to keep in mind:

- Be certain that you have *all* the facts and that they are correct.
- Be brief, giving only the essential information.
- Tell who or what is involved.
- State the occasion.
- Give the exact time it will occur.
- Tell where it will take place, and give clear, specific directions to the location, if it is necessary.
- Repeat the most important facts.
- Speak loudly, distinctly, slowly, and with enthusiasm.

CHAPTER 34

PRAYING IN PUBLIC

PRAYING IN public is an assignment that many people are reluctant to assume. It is, indeed, a special kind of prayer in that the person wording the prayer is speaking for the whole group. There are some who feel that a prayer should be spontaneous in nature and not planned. But, if you are inexperienced in praying in public, you may feel the need for preparing in advance, since you are to assume the responsibility of directing the prayerful thoughts of others toward God.

Preparing to pray will give you self-confidence and lessen your nervousness. Even the apostles felt the need to learn how to pray. In Luke 11:1 they made this request, "Lord, teach us to pray." Jesus gave us the following guidelines for praying effectively in Matthew 6:5–13.

> And when you pray, you shall not be like the hypocrites. For they love to pray standing in the synagogues and on the corners of the streets, that they may be seen by men. Assuredly, I say to you, they have their reward. But you, when you pray, go into your room, and when you have shut your door, pray to your Father who is in the secret place; and your Father who sees in secret will reward you openly. But when you pray, do not use vain repetitions as the heathen do. For they think that they will be heard for their many words.

Therefore do not be like them. For your Father knows the things you have need of before you ask Him. In this manner, therefore, pray:

Our Father in heaven,
hallowed be Your name.
Your kingdom come.
Your will be done
on earth as it is in heaven.
Give us this day our daily bread.
And forgive us our debts,
as we forgive our debtors.
And do not lead us into temptation,
but deliver us from the evil one.
For Yours is the kingdom and the
power and the glory forever.
Amen.

Jesus provided this prayer as a model for our use. It is simple and complete. By studying it, we can arrive at certain standards that apply not only to private prayer, but also to praying in public.

• Direct your prayer to God, using any one of the names of God: Father, Our Heavenly Father, Almighty God, Jehovah God, Dear God, or Father.

• Don't let your prayer be a recounting of events as though God is unaware of them.

• Remember that you are directing the thoughts of others toward God and that you should not word your prayer to impress your human listeners, but you should speak to God about the needs of the group you represent.

• Offer praise to God.

• Express thanksgiving for specific or general blessings granted by God.

• Acknowledge our shortcomings.

• Make requests for God's help.

• Offer the prayer in the name of Jesus, using any one of His names—Jesus, Christ, the Lord, or others.

The following guidelines will also be useful to you in preparing to pray in public:

• Keep your prayer brief.
• Choose your words to fit the occasions, and include those who are praying with you.
• Speak loudly enough and clearly enough to be heard and understood by everyone present.
• Write out your prayer and practice reading it until you have almost memorized it.
• Read your prayer if you feel more comfortable doing that, or refer to your notes to give confidence.

William Hobby offers the following suggestions for praying in specific situations:

• Thanks for food. Keep it simple, but not as brief as the hungry worker's, "Thank you Lord for the vittles, Amen."
1. At home.
a. Thanks for the food is basic.
b. Anything else you wish to include is subject to your desires, such as health, safety of family members, thanks for individual or general blessings. All of these included items would be personal to the one praying and/or to others at the table and probably would not be included in a more public prayer.
Example:
"Father, we thank thee for this food, for each other, and thy many other blessings to us. Bless those we love. Through Christ we pray, Amen."
2. When you are a guest.
a. Thanks for the hospitality and/or friendship with the hosts and other guests.
b. Acknowledgment of occasion for being together.

c. Thanks for the food.

3. At a picnic or covered-dish dinner.

a. Thanks or acknowledgment of the occasion and opportunity for assembling.

b. Thanks for the interest of the group and group activities.

c. Thanks for the food.

d. Appreciation of the ones who prepared the food.

4. At a large formal luncheon or dinner, where the food is bought or catered.

a. Thanks for the occasion of meeting.

b. Thanks for the purpose and interest of the group. Example: honoring someone, homecoming, etc.

c. Hope for the future success of the group's efforts.

d. Thanks for the food.

e. Dedication of selves to God's service.

• Opening a meeting. Similar to No. 4 above without reference to food, d or e. Substitute for c....

• Dismissal or closing prayer.

a. Thanksgiving for the occasion, the time spent, and the blessings received.

b. Petition for safety in separation.

c. For His watchcare in daily life.

d. For safe return to serve.

Do not review the events of the meeting or the message of the hour.[1]

The following sample prayers from *A Book of Prayers* by Showalter and Cox will be helpful to you:

a. Merciful Father, help us to remember that our sojourn here is brief and that in the twinkling of an eye we may be called....Grant that we may study thy word earnestly and sincerely and allow the same to direct us. We recall with sadness our past weaknesses. Henceforth, help us to be stronger. Bless, we beseech thee, the ministers of thy word. May their lives be pure, their speech sound and their hearts tender. Bless the fathers and mothers of our land that they may be strong to bring up their children in thy nurture and admonition. Bless the rulers of our fair country and all that are in high places; that we may lead a tranquil and quiet life in all godliness and gravity. Bless our friends, our enemies if such we have, our kindred, and all for whom we should pray—bless them, Father, in accordance with thy wisdom, power, and infinite compassion. May all men come to know that the best thing in life is pure and undefiled religion. Equip us for battle. Prepare us to live. Comfort us in sickness and in death. Give us an eternal home with thee. In the name of him that loved us, and loosed us from our sins by his blood. Amen.

b. Our Father who art in heaven, hallowed be thy name.... It is with a sense of deepest gratitude, of conscious guilt, and of utter helplessness that we come into thy presence. May our guilt be lost in thy tender mercy and our weakness in thy marvelous strength. In the morning of life, may we hear the divine call. May we give unto thee the first fruits of our earthly existence. Help us to love thee supremely and our neighbors as ourselves. Expel from our hearts every thought of hate, envy, greed, and vulgarity. Cause love, peace, joy, and gentleness to grow as lovely flowers and blossom in our lives. May thy reproofs correct us, thy warnings frighten us, and thy promises allure us on to the heavenly land. In the days of health and happiness, may we be humble. May the pains and adversities of life work in us those graces exemplified in the Christ-life. When shadows of death gather about us, O Lord, may we cling to thee. Be thou our guide across the river. Anchor us safely in the harbor of eternal repose. In Jesus' name. Amen.[2]

PART FOUR:

TOPICAL QUOTATIONS
FOR
SPEAKERS

THIS FINAL section serves as a resource for those in the process of gathering information for speech writing. Arranged alphabetically by topic, the selected quotations cover a variety of subjects and can be used for almost any occasion. Whether you are preparing a graduation speech or a devotional for your Bible study group, a well-chosen quotation or biblical reference can enrich your presentation.

ABILITY

You have to take chances for peace, just as you must take chances in war.... The ability to get to the verge without getting into the war is the necessary art. If you try to run away from it, if you are scared to go to the brink, you are lost.

John Foster Dulles

What we do upon some great occasion will probably depend on what we already are; and what we are will be the result of previous years of self-discipline.

H. P. Liddon

Genius...is the capacity to see ten things where the ordinary man sees one, and where the man of talent sees two or three, plus the ability to register that multiple perception in the material of his art.

Ezra Pound

Intelligence is quickness to apprehend as distinct from ability, which is capacity to act wisely on the thing apprehended.

Alfred North Whitehead

ACTION

Every action of our lives touches on some chord that will vibrate in eternity.

E. H. Chapin

Remember, then, that it [science] is the guide of action; that the truth which it arrives at is not that which we can ideally contemplate without error, but that which we may act upon without fear; and you cannot fail to see that scientific thought is not an accompaniment or condition of human progress, but human progress itself.

William Kingdon Clifford

Only actions give to life its strength, as only moderation gives it its charm.

Jean Paul F. Richter

Doing is the great thing. For if, resolutely, people do what is right, in time they come to like doing it.

John Ruskin

AGING

The silver-haired head is a crown of glory,/If it is found in the way of righteousness.

Proverbs 16:31

O God, You have taught me from my youth;
And to this day I declare Your wondrous works.
Now also when I am old and gray-headed,
O God, do not forsake me,
Until I declare Your strength to this generation,
Your power to everyone who is to come.

Psalm 71:17–18

Age in a virtuous person, of either sex, carries in it an authority which makes it preferable to all the pleasures of youth.

Sir Richard Steele

Do not go gentle into that good night,
Old age should burn and rave at close of day;
Rage, rage against the dying of the light.

Dylan Thomas

AMERICA

All I want is the same thing you want. To have a nation with a government that is as good and honest and decent and competent and compassionate and as filled with love as are the American people.

Jimmy Carter

There is nothing wrong with America that the faith, love of freedom, intelligence, and energy of her citizens cannot cure.

Dwight D. Eisenhower

Equal and exact justice to all men, of whatever state or persuasion, religious or political; peace, commerce, and honest friendship with all nations, entangling alliances with none....Freedom of religion; freedom of the press, and freedom of person under the protection of the habeas corpus, and trial by juries impartially selected. These principles form the bright constellation which has gone before us, and guided our steps through an age of revolution and reformation. The wisdom of our sages and the blood of our heroes have been devoted to their attainment. They should be the creed of our political faith, the text of civil instruction, the touchstone by which we try the services of those we trust; and should we wander from them in moments of error or alarm, let us hasten to retrace our steps and to regain the road which alone leads to peace, liberty, and safety.

Thomas Jefferson

The home of freedom, and the hope of the down-trodden and oppressed among the nations of the earth.

Daniel Webster

ANGER

You are God, ready to pardon, gracious and merciful, slow to anger, abundant in kindness.

Nehemiah 9:17

Laugh then at any but at fools or foes;
These you but anger, and you mend not those.
Laugh at your friends, and if your friends are sore,
So much the better, you may laugh the more.
Alexander Pope

Cease from anger, and forsake wrath;/Do not fret—it only causes harm.
Psalm 37:8

A soft answer turns away wrath,
But a harsh word stirs up anger.
A wrathful man stirs up strife,
But he who is slow to anger allays contention.
Proverbs 15:1,18

APPRECIATION

A work of real merit finds favor at last.
Amos Bronson Alcott

It is the lone worker who makes the first advance in a subject: the details may be worked out by a team, but the prime idea is due to the enterprise, thought and perception of an individual.
Sir Alexander Fleming

We are very much what others think of us.—The reception our observations meet with gives us courage to proceed, or damps our efforts.
William Hazlitt

The unfailing formula for production of morale is patriotism, self-respect, discipline, and self-confidence within a military unit, joined with fair treatment and merited appreciation from without....It will quickly wither and die if soldiers come to believe themselves the victims of indifference or injustice on the part of their government, or of ignorance, personal ambition, or ineptitude on the part of their military leader.
Douglas MacArthur

BEAUTY

As a white candle
In a holy place,

So is the beauty
Of an aged face.
Joseph Campbell

Beauty in things exists in the mind which contemplates them.
David Hume

"Beauty is truth, truth beauty,"—that is all/Ye know on earth,
and all ye need to know.
John Keats

Beauty like hers is genius.

Dante Gabriel Rossetti

BELIEF

Be not afraid of life. Believe that life is worth living, and your
belief will help create the fact.
William James

Know you what it is to be a child? It is to be something very different from the man of today. It is to have a spirit yet streaming
from the waters of baptism; it is to believe in love, to believe in
loveliness, to believe in belief; it is to be so little that the elves can
reach to whisper in your ear; it is to turn pumpkins into coaches,
and mice into horses, lowness into loftiness, and nothing into everything, for each child has its fairy godmother in its soul.
Francis Thompson

Some believe all that parents, tutors, and kindred believe.—
They take their principles by inheritance, and defend them as they
would their estates, because they are born heirs to them.
Isaac Watts

One in whom persuasion and belief
Had ripened into faith, and faith become
A passionate intuition.
William Wordsworth

BENEVOLENCE

The heart benevolent and kind
The most resembles God.

Robert Burns

Always on Monday morning the press reports
God as revealed to His vicars in various guises—
Benevolent, stormy, patient, or out of sorts.
God knows which God is the God God recognizes.
                                          Phyllis McGinley

To feel much for others, and little for ourselves; to restrain our selfish, and exercise our benevolent affections, constitutes the perfection of human nature.
                                          Adam Smith

Peace is not an absence of war, it is a virtue, a state of mind, a disposition for benevolence, confidence, justice.
                                          Benedict [Baruch] Spinoza

BRAVERY

Bravery never goes out of fashion.
                                          Robert Browning

Watch, stand fast in the faith, be brave, be strong.
                                          1 Corinthians 16:13

True bravery is shown by performing without witnesses what one might be capable of doing before all the world.
                                          Duc Francois de La Rochefoucauld

The best hearts are ever the bravest.
                                          Lawrence Sterne

BREVITY

Have something to say; say it, and stop when you've done.
                                          Tryon Edwards

Genuine good taste consists in saying much in few words, in choosing among our thoughts, in having order and arrangement in what we say, and in speaking with composure.
                                          Francois Fenelon

Talk to the point, and stop when you have reached it.—Be comprehensive in all you say or write.—To fill a volume about nothing is a credit to nobody.
                                          John Neal

Brevity is the soul of wit.

William Shakespeare

BUSINESS

The chief business of the American people is business.
Calvin Coolidge

The best business you can go into you will find on your father's farm or in his workshop. If you have no family or friends to aid you, and no prospect opened to you there, turn your face to the great West, and there build up a home and fortune.

Horace Greeley

That one hundred and fifty lawyers should do business together ought not to be expected.

Thomas Jefferson

If they obey and serve Him, they shall spend their days in prosperity, and their years in pleasures.

Job 36:11

CAUTION

Cautious, careful people, always casting about to preserve their reputation and social standing, never can bring about a reform. Those who are really in earnest must be willing to be anything or nothing in the world's estimation.

Susan Brownell Anthony

I don't like these cold, precise, perfect people, who, in order not to speak wrong, never speak at all, and in order not to do wrong, never do anything.

H. W. Beecher

The cautious seldom err.

Confucius

The scars of others should teach us caution.
St. Jerome

CENSORSHIP

If censorship reigns there cannot be sincere flattery, and only small men are afraid of small writings.

Pierre de Beaumarchais

So many new ideas are at first strange and horrible though ultimately valuable that a very heavy responsibility rests upon those who would prevent their dissemination.

J.B.S. Haldane

Mankind censure injustice fearing that they may be the victims of it, and not because they shrink from committing it.

Plato

Assassination is the extreme form of censorship.

George Bernard Shaw

CHARITY

Liberty like charity must begin at home.

James Bryant Conant

Though I have all faith, so that I could remove mountains, and have not charity, I am nothing.

And though I bestow all my goods to feed the poor, and though I give my body to be burned, and have not charity, it profiteth me nothing.

Charity suffereth long, and is kind; charity envieth not; charity vaunteth not itself, is not puffed up.

1 Corinthians 13:2–4

The charity that hastens to proclaim its good deeds ceases to be charity, and is only pride and ostentation.

Hutton

Charity creates a multitude of sins.

Wilde

CHEERFULNESS

What sunshine is to flowers, smiles are to humanity. They are but trifles, to be sure; but, scattered along life's pathway, the good they do is inconceivable.

Author Unknown

I have tried too in my time to be a philosopher; but I don't know how, cheerfulness was always breaking in.

Oliver Edwards

The true source of cheerfulness is benevolence.—The soul that perpetually overflows with kindness and sympathy will always be cheerful.

P. Godwin

Honest good humor is the oil and wine of a merry meeting, and there is no jovial companionship equal to that where the jokes are rather small and the laughter abundant.

Washington Irving

CHILDREN

There are few things more pitiful than a grown man out of whom all the boy has died.

Bascon Anthony

If I were asked what single qualification was necessary for one who has the care of children, I should say patience—patience with their tempers, with their understandings, with their progress. It is not brilliant parts or great acquirements which are necessary for teachers, but patience to go over first principles again and again; steadily to add a little every day; never to be irritated by willful or accidental hinderance.

Francois Fenelon

Children are God's apostles, sent forth, day by day, to preach of love, and hope, and peace.

J. R. Lowell

Every child born into the world is a new thought of God, an every-fresh and radiant possibility.

Kate Douglas Wiggin

CHURCH

The First Amendment has erected a wall between church and state. That wall must be kept high and impregnable. We could not approve the slightest breach.

Hugo LaFayette Black

For no one ever hated his own flesh, but nourishes and cherishes it, just as the Lord does the church. For we are members of His body, of His flesh and of His bones.

Ephesians 5:29–30

And He put all things under His feet, and gave Him to be head over all things to the church, which is His body, the fullness of Him who fills all in all.

Ephesians 1:22–23

I always love to begin a journey on Sundays, because I shall have the prayers of the church to preserve all that travel by land, or by water.

Jonathan Swift

CITIZENSHIP

Neither democracy nor effective representation is possible until each participant in the group—and this is true equally of a household or a nation—devotes a measurable part of his life to furthering its existence.

Lewis Mumford

Voting is the least arduous of a citizen's duties. He has the prior and harder duty of making up his mind.

Ralph Barton Perry

As citizens of this democracy, you are the rulers and the ruled, the lawgivers and the law-abiding, the beginning and the end.

Adlai Stevenson

Our "pathway" is straight to the ballot box, with no variableness, no shadow of turning....We demand in the Reconstruction suffrage for all the citizens of the Republic. I would not talk of Negroes or women, but of citizens.

Elizabeth Cady Stanton

COOPERATION

Today it is generally recognized that all corporations possess an element of public interest. A corporation director must think not only of the stockholder but also of the laborer, the supplier, the purchaser, and the ultimate consumer. Our economy is but a chain which can be no stronger than any one of its links. We all stand together or fall together in our highly industrialized society of today.

William O. Douglas

Fundamentally, there are only two ways of coordinating the economic activities of millions. One is central direction involving the use of coercion—the technique of the army and of the modern totalitarian state. The other is voluntary cooperation of individuals—the technique of the marketplace.

Milton Friedman

Universal experience teaches us that no nation has ever yet risen from want and poverty to a better and loftier station without the unremitting toil of all its citizens, both employers and employed. …Unless brains, capital and labor combine together for common effort, men's toil cannot produce due fruit.

Pope Pius XI

The highest and best form of efficiency is the spontaneous cooperation of a free people.

Woodrow Wilson

COURAGE

The brave man is not he who feels no fear, for that were stupid and irrational; but he whose noble soul subdues its fear, and bravely dares the danger nature shrinks from.

Joanna Baillie

To see what is right and not to do it, is want of courage.

Confucius

The bravest thing you can do when you are not brave is to profess courage and act accordingly.

Corra Harris

True courage is not the brutal force of vulgar heroes, but the firm resolve of virtue and reason.

Paul Whitehead

COURTESY

The courtesies of a small and trivial character are the ones which strike deepest to the grateful and appreciating heart. It is the picayune compliments which are the most appreciated; far more than the double ones we sometimes pay.

Henry Clay

There is no outward sign of true courtesy that does not rest on a deep moral foundation.

Johann Wolfgang von Goethe

When saluted with a salutation, salute the person with a better salutation, or at least return the same, for God taketh account of all things.

The Koran

Courtesy is a science of the highest importance.—It is like grace and beauty in the body, which charm at first sight, and lead on to further intimacy and friendship.

Michel de Montaigne

CREATION

God creates out of nothing. Wonderful, you say. Yes, to be sure, but He does what is still more wonderful: He makes saints out of sinners.

Soren Kierkegaard

The heavens declare the glory of God; And the firmament shows His handiwork.

Psalm 19:1

The earth is the LORD's. And all its fullness,
The world and those who dwell therein.
For He has founded it upon the seas,
And established it upon the waters.

Psalm 24:1–2

You are worthy, O Lord, to receive glory and honor and power; for You created all things, and by Your will they exist and were created.

Revelation 4:11

DEEDS

Our deeds follow us, and what we have been makes us what we are.

Author Unknown

Our deeds determine us, as much as we determine our deeds.
George Eliot

A word that has been said may be unsaid—it is but air.—But when a deed is done, it cannot be undone, nor can our thoughts reach out to all the mischiefs that may follow.
Henry Longfellow

Look on little deeds as great, on account of Christ, who dwells in us, and watches our life; look on great deeds as easy, on account of His great power.
Blaise Pascal

DEMOCRACY

The country still has faith in the rule of the people it's going to elect next.
Ted Cook

Human dignity, economic freedom, individual responsibility, these are the characteristics that distinguish democracy from all other forms devised by man.
Dwight D. Eisenhower

Of the many things we have done to democracy in the past, the worst has been the indignity of taking it for granted.
Max Lerner

Democracy, the practice of self-government, is a covenant among free men to respect the rights and liberties of their fellows.
Franklin D. Roosevelt

DIGNITY

The basic tenet of black consciousness is that the black man must reject all value systems that seek to make him a foreigner in the country of his birth and reduce his basic human dignity.
Steve Biko

We must build a new world, a far better world—one in which the eternal dignity of man is respected.
Norman Mattoon Thomas

If man is not ready to risk his life, where is his dignity?
André Malraux

No race can prosper till it learns that there is as much dignity in tilling a field as in writing a poem.

Booker T. Washington

DILIGENCE

In all departments of activity, to have one thing to do, and then to do it, is the secret of success.

Author Unknown

What we hope ever to do with ease, we must learn first to do with diligence.

Johnson

He who labors diligently need never despair; for all things are accomplished by diligence and labor.

Menander

Diligence is the mother of good luck, and God gives all things to industry. Work while it is called to-day, for you know not how much you may be hindered to-morrow. One to-day is worth two to-morrows; never leave that till to-morrow which you can do to-day.

Ben Franklin

DUTY

The best things are nearest: light in your eyes, flowers at your feet, duties at your hand, the path of God just before you. Then do not grasp at the stars, but do life's common work as it comes, certain that daily duties and daily bread are the sweetest things of life.

God always has an angel of help for those who are willing to do their duty.

T. L. Cuyler

We do not choose our own parts in life, and have nothing to do with selecting those parts. Our simple duty is confined to playing them well.

Epictetus

Reverence the highest; have patience with the lowest; let this day's performance of the meanest duty be thy religion.

Margaret Fuller

Do thy duty; that is best; leave unto the Lord the rest.
Henry Longfellow

EDUCATION

The whole object of education is, or should be, to develop the mind. The mind should be a thing that works. It should be able to pass judgment on events as they arise, make decisions.
Sherwood Anderson

The secret of education lies in respecting the pupil.
Ralph Waldo Emerson

I have never met a man so ignorant that I couldn't learn something from him.
Galileo

States should spend money and effort on this great all-underlying matter of spiritual education as they have hitherto spent them on beating and destroying each other.
John Galsworthy

ENCOURAGEMENT

And let us not grow weary while doing good, for in due season we shall reap if we do not lose heart.
Galatians 6:9

Though I walk in the midst of trouble, You will revive me;
You will stretch out Your hand
Against the wrath of my enemies,
And Your right hand will save me.
Psalm 138:7

Faint not; the miles to heaven are but few and short.
Joseph Franklin Rutherford

You know, Lord, how many things I begin.
You know how many go unfinished.
At times my life seems to be a tangle of loose ends.
What you begin you complete, even while you continue creating.
How you can finish and continue at the same time is beyond me.

But I know you are doing it in us and in our world.

Joyce Blackburn

ENTHUSIASM

Enlist the interests of stern morality and religious enthusiasm in the cause of political liberty, as in the time of the old Puritans, and it will be irresistible.

Samuel T. Coleridge

Every production of genius must be the production of enthusiasm.

Benjamin Disraeli

Truth is never to be expected from authors whose understanding are warped with enthusiasm; for they judge all actions and their causes by their own perverse principles, and a crooked line can never be the measure of a straight one.

John Dryden

The sense of this word among the Greeks affords the noblest definition of it; enthusiasm signifies "God in us."

Madame de Staël

EXAMPLE

Not the cry, but the flight of the wild duck, leads the flock to fly and follow.

Chinese Proverb

Of all commentaries upon the Scriptures, good examples are the best and the liveliest.

John Donne

The conscience of children is formed by the influences that surround them; their notions of good and evil are the result of the atmosphere they breathe.

Jean Paul Richter

Live with wolves, and you will learn to howl.

Spanish Proverb

EXCELLENCE

They are the lords and owners of their faces,

Others but stewards of their excellence.
The summer's flower is to the summer sweet,
Though to itself it only live and die.
William Shakespeare

The renown which riches or beauty confer is fleeting and frail;
mental excellence is a splendid and lasting possession.
Sallust [Gaius Sallustius Crispus]

It takes a long time to bring excellence to maturity.
Publilius Syrus

What is our praise or pride
But to imagine excellence, and try to make it?
What does it say over the door of Heaven
But *homo fecit*?
Richard Purdy Wilbur

EXPERIENCE

Experience—making all futures, fruits of all the pasts.
Arnold

Experience, that chill touchstone whose sad proof reduces all
things from their false hue.
George Gordon, Lord Byron

Experience takes dreadfully high school-wages, but he teaches
like no other.
Thomas Carlyle

I know the past, and thence will assay to glean a warning for the
future, so that man may profit by his errors, and derive experience
from his folly.
Percy Bysshe Shelley

FAITH

Feed your faith, and your doubts will starve to death.
Author Unknown

For whatever is born of God overcomes the world. And this is
the victory that has overcome the world—our faith.
1 John 5:4

Faith, as I see it, simply connects us to Him in all His mystery and wonder and love.

Eugenia Price

Faith is the bird that sings while dawn is still dark.

Rabindranath Tagore

FAMILY

Happy are the families where the government of parents is the reign of affection, and obedience of the children the submission of love.

If I might control the literature of the household, I would guarantee the well-being of the church and state.

Francis Bacon

If God has taught us all truth in teaching us to love, then he has given us an interpretation of our whole duty to our households.— We are not born as the partridge in the wood, or the ostrich of the desert, to be scattered everywhere; but we are to be grouped together, and brooded by love, and reared day by day in that first of churches, the family.

H. W. Beecher

A happy family is but an earlier heaven.

Bowring

As are families, so is society.—If well ordered, well instructed, and well governed, they are the springs from which go forth the streams of national greatness and prosperity—of civil order and public happiness.

Thayer

FATHER

Again, men in general desire the good, and not merely what their fathers had.

Aristotle

Becoming a father is easy enough,
But being one can be rough.

Wilhelm Busch

Fathers, provoke not your children to anger, lest they be discouraged.

> Colossians 3:21

Let us now praise famous men and our fathers that begat us.

> Ecclesiasticus 44:1

FREEDOM

Freedom is not worth having if it does not connote freedom to err.

> Gandhi

Freedom of religion, freedom of the press, and freedom of person under the protection of the habeaus corpus, these are principles that have guided our steps through an age of revolution and reformation.

> Thomas Jefferson

Many politicians lay it down as a self-evident proposition, that no people ought to be free till they are fit to use their freedom.—The maxim is worthy of the fool in the old story, who resolved not to go into the water till he had learned to swim.

> Thomas Macaulay

When an American says that he loves his country, he...means that he loves an inner air, an inner light in which freedom lives and in which a man can draw the breath of self-respect.

> Adlai Stevenson

FRIENDSHIP

When I see an honored friend again after years of separation, it is like resuming the words of an old conversation which had been halted momentarily by time. Surely as one gets older, friendship becomes more precious to us, for it affirms the contours of our existence. It is a reservoir of shared experience, of having lived through many things in our brief and mutual moment on earth.

> Willie Morris

A man who has friends must himself be friendly,
But there is a friend who sticks closer than a brother.

> Proverbs 18:24

Friendship—one soul in two bodies.

Pythagoras

Friendship is to be purchased only by friendship. A man may have authority over others, but he can never have their heart but by giving his own.

Thomas Wilson

GENEROSITY

We enjoy thoroughly only the pleasure that we give.

Alexander Dumas

It is better to give than to lend, and it costs about the same.

Sir Philip Gibbs

You are so to give, and to sacrifice to give, as to earn the eulogium pronounced on the woman, "She hath done what she could."—Do it now.—It is not safe to leave a generous feeling to the cooling influences of a cold world.

Guthrie

We should give as we would receive cheerfully, quickly, and without hesitation; for there is no grace in a benefit that sticks to the fingers.

Seneca

GIFTS

He who loves with purity considers not the gift of the lover, but the love of the giver.

Thomas á Kempis

The heart of the giver makes the gift dear and precious.

Martin Luther

Every gift, though it be small, is in reality great if given with affection.

Pindar

That which is given with pride and ostentation is rather an ambition than a bounty.

Seneca

GOVERNMENT

Our civilization has decided, and very justly decided, that determining the guilt or innocence of men is a thing too important to be trusted to trained men. When it wishes for light upon that awful matter, it asks men who know no more law than I know, but who can feel the things that I felt in the jury box. When it wants a library catalogued, or the solar system discovered, or any trifle of that kind, it uses up its specialists. But when it wishes anything done which is really serious, it collects twelve of the ordinary men standing round. The same thing was done, if I remember right, by the Founder of Christianity.

G. K. Chesterton

There are those, I know, who will say that the liberation of humanity, the freedom of man and mind, is nothing but a dream. They are right. It is. It is the American dream.

Archibald MacLeish

Render therefore to all their due: taxes to whom taxes are due, customs to whom customs, fear to whom fear, honor to whom honor.

Romans 13:7

Remind them to be subject to rulers and authorities, to obey, to be ready for every good work, to speak evil of no one, to be peaceable, gentle, showing all humility to all men.

Titus 3:1–2

GRATITUDE

To the generous mind the heaviest debt is that of gratitude, when it is not in our power to repay it.

Ben Franklin

A grateful thought toward heaven is of itself a prayer.

Gotthold Lessing

We can be thankful to a friend for a few acres or a little money; and yet for the freedom and command of the whole earth, and for the great benefits of our being, our life, health, and reason, we look upon ourselves as under no obligation.

Seneca

From David learn to give thanks for everything. Every furrow in the Book of Psalms is sown with the seeds of thanksgiving.

Jeremy Taylor

GREATNESS

No man has come to true greatness who has not felt in some degree that his life belongs to his race, and that what God gives him he gives him for mankind.

Phillips Brooks

It is easy in the world to live after the world's opinion—it is easy in solitude to live after your own; but the great man is he who, in the midst of the world, keeps with perfect sweetness the independence of solitude.

Ralph Waldo Emerson

If any man seeks for greatness, let him forget greatness and ask for truth, and he will find both.

Horace Mann

Not a day passes over the earth but men and women of no note do great deeds, speak great words, and suffer noble sorrows. Of these obscure heroes, philosophers, and martyrs the greater part will never be known till that hour when many that were great shall be small, and the small great.

Charles Reade

HAPPINESS

The Greeks said grandly in their tragic phrase, "Let no one be called happy till his death"; to which I would add, "Let no one, till his death, be called unhappy."

Elizabeth B. Browning

Happiness is a sunbeam which may pass through a thousand bosoms without losing a particle of its original ray; nay, when it strikes on a kindred heart, like the light on a mirror, it reflects itself with redoubled brightness.—It is not perfected till it is shared.

Jane Porter

Blessed is every one who fears the LORD,
Who walks in His ways.

When you eat the labor of your hands,
You shall be happy, and it shall be well with you.
Psalm 128:1-2

The fountain of content must spring up in the mind, and he who has so little knowledge of human nature as to seek happiness by changing anything but his own disposition will waste his life in fruitless efforts and multiply the griefs which he purposes to remove.
Samuel Johnson

HEROISM

Heroes in history seem to us poetic because they are there.—But if we should tell the simple truth of some of our neighbors, it would sound like poetry.
G. W. Curtis

Self-trust is the essence of heroism.
Ralph Waldo Emerson

However great the advantages which nature bestows on us, it is not she alone, but fortune in conjunction with her, which makes heroes.
Francois de La Rochefoucauld

Heroes are not known by the loftiness of their carriage; the greatest braggarts are generally the merest cowards.
Jean Jacques Rousseau

HOLIDAYS

Let your holidays be associated with great public events, and they may be the life of patriotism as well as a source of relaxation and personal employment.
Tryon Edwards

The holiest of all holidays are those kept by ourselves in silence and apart, the secret anniversaries of the heart, when the full tide of feeling overflows.
Henry Longfellow

Under the leaves, amid the grass, lazily the day shall pass, yet not be wasted.—From my drowsy ease I borrow health and strength to bear my boat through the great life ocean.

Mackay

If all the year were playing holidays, to sport would be as tedious as to work; but when they seldom come, the wished for come.

William Shakespeare

HOME

America's future will be determined by the home and the school. The child becomes largely what it is taught, hence we must watch what we teach it, and how we live before it.

Jane Addams

Home is the seminary of all other institutions.

E. H. Chapin

The most essential element in any home is God.

Frank Crane

Christianity begins at home. We build our characters there, and what we become in after years is largely determined by our training and home environment.

Tillman Hobson

HONESTY

If honesty did not exist, we ought to invent it as the best means of getting rich.

Comte de Mirabeau

It would be an unspeakable advantage, both to the public and private, if men would consider the great truth, that no man is wise or safe, but he that is honest.

Sir Walter Raleigh

The shortest and surest way to live with honor in the world, is to be in reality what we would appear to be; and if we observe, we shall find, that all human virtues increase and strengthen themselves by the practice and experience of them.

Socrates

I hope I shall always possess firmness and virtue enough to maintain what I consider the most enviable of all titles, the character of an honest man.

George Washington

HONOR

Honor is like the eye, which cannot suffer the least impurity without damage.—It is a precious stone, the price of which is lessened by a single flaw.

Jacques Bossuet

Our own heart, and not other men's opinion, forms our true honor.

Samuel Taylor Coleridge

For the fruits of honor are courtesy, gentleness, integrity, and charity. Honor is the only tree on which all the virtues grow.

Archibald Rutledge

Life every man holds dear; but the dear man holds honor far more precious dear than life.

William Shakespeare

HOPE

Cling to the flying hours; and yet let one pure hope, one great desire, like song on dying lips be set—that ere we fall in scattered fire our hearts may lift the world's heart higher.

Edmund W. Gosse

My country owes me nothing. It gave me, as it gives every boy and girl, a chance. It gave me schooling, independence of action, opportunity for service and honor. In no other land could a boy from a country village, without inheritance or influential friends, look forward with unbounded hope.

Herbert Hoover

For You are my hope, O Lord GOD:
You are my trust from my youth.

Psalm 71:5

For whatever things were written before were written for our learning, that we through the patience and comfort of the Scriptures might have hope.

Romans 15:4

HUMOR

We love a joke that hands us a pat on the back while it kicks the other fellow down stairs.

C. L. Edson

A man isn't poor if he can still laugh.

Raymond Hitchcock

With the fearful strain that is on me night and day, if I did not laugh I should die.

Abraham Lincoln

Good humor is one of the best articles of dress one can wear in society.

William Thackeray

HUSBAND

It is easier to be a lover than a husband for the simple reason that it is more difficult to be witty every day than to say pretty things from time to time.

Honoré de Balzac

Being a husband is a whole-time job.

Eroch Arnold Bennett

May the gods grant you all things which your heart desires, and may they give you a husband and a home and gracious concord.

Homer

Let still the woman take
An elder than herself, so wears she to him,
So sways she level in her husband's heart:
For, boy, however we do praise ourselves,
Our fancies are more giddy and unfirm,
More longing, wavering, sooner lost and worn,
Than women's are.

William Shakespeare

IDEALISM

The attainment of an ideal is often the beginning of a disillusion.

Stanley Baldwin

The "liberal" of our times has become all too often little more than a sentimentalist "with both feet planted firmly in mid-air."

Louis Bromfield

No folly is more costly than the folly of intolerant idealism.

Winston Churchill

Words without actions are the assassins of idealism.

Herbert Hoover

IDEALS

The best and noblest lives are those which are set toward high ideals. And the highest and noblest ideal that any man can have is Jesus of Nazareth.

Rene Almeras

We never reach our ideals, whether of mental or moral improvement, but the thought of them shows us our deficiencies, and spurs us on to higher and better things.

Tryon Edwards

It is a welcome symptom in an age which is commonly denounced as materialistic, that it makes heroes of men whose goals lie wholly in the intellectual and moral sphere. This proves that knowledge and justice are ranked above wealth and power by a large section of the human race.... This idealistic outlook is particularly prevalent in America, which is decried as a singularly materialistic country.

Albert Einstein

A man's ideal, like his horizon, is constantly receding from him as he advances toward it.

W. G. T. Shedd

IDEAS

Events are only the shells of ideas; and often it is the fluent thought of ages that is crystallized in a moment by the stroke of a pen or the point of a bayonet.

E. H. Chapin

Ideas make their way in silence like the waters that, filtering behind the rocks of the Alps, loosen them from the mountains on which they rest.

Charles Francois D'Aubigné

An idea, like a ghost, according to the common notion of ghosts, must be spoken to a little before it will explain itself.

Charles Dickens

To have ideas is to gather flowers; to think, is to weave them into garlands.

Madame Swetchine

IMAGINATION

Thought convinces; feeling persuades.—If imagination furnishes the fact with wings, feeling is the great, stout muscle which plies them, and lifts him from the ground.—Thought sees beauty; emotion feels it.

Theodore Parker

Imagination disposes of everything; it creates beauty, justice, and happiness, which are everything in this world.

Blaise Pascal

The world of reality has its limits; the world of imagination is boundless.—Not being able to enlarge the one, let us contract the other; for it is from their difference that all the evils arise which render us unhappy.

Jean Jacques Rousseau

The human race built most nobly when limitations were greatest and, therefore, when most was required of imagination in order to build at all. Limitations seem to have always been the best friends of architecture.

Frank Lloyd Wright

INDEPENDENCE

The word independence is united to the ideas of dignity and virtue; the word dependence, to the ideas of inferiority and corruption.

Jeremy Betham

There is often as much independence in not being led, as in not being driven.

Tryon Edwards

The greatest of all human benefits, that, at least, without which no other benefit can be truly enjoyed, is independence.

Parke Godwin

The moral progression of a people can scarcely begin till they are independent.

James Martineau

INDIVIDUALITY

We live too much in platoons; we march by sections; we do not live in our individuality enough; we are slaves to fashion in mind and heart, if not to our passions and appetites.

E. H. Chapin

Every individual nature has its own beauty.—In every company, at every fireside, one is struck with the riches of nature, when he hears so many tones, all musical, sees in each person original manners which have a proper and peculiar charm, and reads new expressions of face.—He perceives that nature has laid for each the foundations of a divine building if the soul will build thereon.

Ralph Waldo Emerson

The common phrase, "building a personality" is a misnomer.— Personality is not so much like a structure as like a river—it continuously flows, and to be a person is to be engaged in a perpetual process of becoming.

Harry Emerson Fosdick

The worth of a state, in the long run, is the worth of the individuals composing it.

John Stuart Mill

INTEGRITY

Nothing more completely baffles who is full of trick and duplic-

ity, than straightforward and simple integrity in another.
                                                    Colton

Nothing is at last sacred but the integrity of your own mind.
Absolve you to yourself, and you shall have the suffrage of the
world.
                                        Ralph Waldo Emerson

In all things preserve integrity; and the consciousness of thine
own uprightness will alleviate the toil of business, soften the hard-
ness of ill-success and disappointments, and give thee an humble
confidence before God, when the ingratitude of man, or the in-
iquity of the times may rob thee of other reward.
                                            William Paley

Integrity without knowledge is weak and useless.
Undoubtedly, there is little integration or integrity in most
men's characters; there is only habit and a plodding limitation in
life and mind; and if social pressure were not added to lack of opportunity disorderly lives would be more common than they are.
                                        George Santayana

INTELLECT

Intelligence increases mere physical ability one half.—The use
of the head abridges the labor of the hands.
                                            H.W. Beecher

The more we know of any one ground of knowledge, the further
we see into the general domains of intellect.
                                            Leigh Hunt

God multiplies intelligence, which communicates itself like
fire, infinitely.—Light a thousand torches at one torch, and the
flame of the latter remains the same.
                                        Petrus Joubert

Mind is the greater lever of all things; human thought is the
process by which human ends are answered.
                                        Daniel Webster

INTENTIONS

In the works of man as in those of nature, it is the intention which is chiefly worth studying.

Johann Wolfgang von Goethe

Many good purposes and intentions lie in the churchyard.

Philip Henry

Good intention will no more make a truth, than a good mark will make a good shot.

Spurstowe

Right intention is to the actions of a man what the soul is to the body, or the root to the tree.

Jeremy Taylor

JOY

Great joy, especially after a sudden change of circumstances, is apt to be silent, and dwells rather in the heart than on the tongue.

Henry Fielding

To pursue joy is to lose it. The only way to get it is to follow steadily the path of duty, without thinking of joy, and then, like sheep, it comes most surely unsought, and we "bring in the way," the angel of God, bright-haired Joy, is sure to meet us.

A. Maclaren

Praise the LORD with the harp;
Make melody to Him with an instrument
　　of ten strings.
Sing to Him a new song;
Play skillfully with a shout of joy.

Psalm 33:1

"Shared joy is double joy and shared sorrow is half-sorrow."

Swedish Proverb

JUSTICE

Justice shines in smoky cottages, and honors the pious. Leaving with averted eyes the gorgeous glare obtained by polluted hands, she is wont to draw nigh to holiness, not reverencing wealth when falsely stamped with praise, and assigning to each deed its righteous doom.

Aeschulus

Justice is as strictly due between neighbor nations, as between neighbor citizens. A highwayman is as much a robber when he plunders in a gang, as when single; and a nation that makes an unjust war is only a great gang of robbers.

Ben Franklin

God's mill grinds slow but sure.

George Herbert

The only way to make the mass of mankind see the beauty of justice, is by showing them, in pretty plain terms, the consequence of injustice.

Sydney Smith

KINDNESS

Kindness is a language the dumb can speak, and the deaf can hear and understand.

Bovee

To cultivate kindness is a valuable part of the business of life.

Samuel Johnson

I expect to pass through life but once.—If therefore, there be any kindness I can show, or any good thing I can do to any fellow-being, let me do it now, and not defer or neglect it, as I shall not pass this way again.

William Penn

Sow good services; sweet remembrances will grow from them.

Madame de Staël

KNOWLEDGE

Reading maketh a full man; conference, a ready man: histories make men wise; poets, witty; the mathematics, subtle; natural philosophy, deep; moral philosophy, grave; logic and rhetoric, able to contend.

Francis Bacon

"Know thyself" means this, that you get acquainted with what you know, and what you can do.

Menander

The end of all learning is to know God, and out of that knowledge to love and imitate him.

John Milton

The desire of knowledge, like the thirst of riches, increases ever with the acquisition of it.

Laurence Sterne

LAUGHTER

A laugh, to be joyous, must flow from a joyous heart, for without kindness there can be no true joy.

The most utterly lost of all days, is that in which you have not once laughed.

Chamfort

Men show their character in nothing more clearly than by what they think laughable.

Johann Wolfgang von Goethe

Man is the only creature endowed with the power of laughter; is he not also the only one that deserves to be laughed at?

Greville

LEARNING

Wear your learning, like your watch, in a private pocket.—Do not pull it out merely to show that you have one.—If asked what o'clock it is, tell it; but do not proclaim it hourly and unasked, like the watchman.

Earl of Chesterfield

He might have been a very clever man by nature, but he had laid so many books on his head that his brain could not move.

Robert Hall

The learning and knowledge that we have, is, at the most, but little compared with that of which we are ignorant.

Plato

A little learning is a dangerous thing! Drink deep, or taste not the Pierian spring; there shallow draughts intoxicate the brain, and drinking largely sobers us again.

Alexander Pope

LIBERTY

No free government, or the blessings of liberty can be preserved to any people but by a firm adherence to justice, moderation, temperance, frugality, and virtue, and by a frequent recurrence to fundamental principles.

Patrick Henry

There are two freedoms, the false where one is free to do what he likes, and the true where he is free to do what he ought.

C. Kingsley

The principle of liberty and equality, if coupled with mere selfishness, will make men only devils, each trying to be independent that he may fight only for his own interest.—And here is the need of religion and its power, to bring in the principle of benevolence and love to men.

John Randolph

If the true spark of religious and civil liberty be kindled, it will burn. Human agency cannot extinguish it. Like the earth's central fire, it may be smothered for a time; the ocean may overwhelm it; mountains may press it down; but its inherent and unconquerable force will heave both the ocean and the land, and at some time or another, in some place or another, the volcano will break out and flame to heaven.

Daniel Webster

LOVE

Maybe we simply need to know what we care about.

If we put a high value on decency, if we put a high value on excellence and on family, if we love the people we share our lives with—our wives and our husbands, our children—and if we don't shortchange them for a few bucks, if we can love the work we do and learn the skill of it, the art of it, if we can give full measure to the people who pay us for our work, if we try not to lie, try not to cheat, try to do good just by doing well whatever we do...then we will have made a revolution.

Alan Alda

If love is blind, marriage must be a real eye-opener.
                                            Author Unknown

And the LORD God said, "It is not good that man should be alone; I will make him a helper comparable to him.". . . Therefore a man shall leave his father and mother and be joined to his wife, and they shall become one flesh.
                                            Genesis 2:18, 24

"Love cures people—both the ones who give it and the ones who receive it."
                                            Dr. Carl Menninger

MARRIAGE

Marriage, to women as to men, must be a luxury, not a necessity; an incident of life, not all of it. And the only possible way to accomplish this great change is to accord to women equal power in the making, shaping and controlling of the circumstances of life.
                                            Susan B. Anthony

Married in haste, we repent at leisure.
                                            William Congreve

One of the good things that come of a true marriage is, that there is one face on which changes come without your seeing them; or rather there is one face which you can still see the same, through all the shadows which years have gathered upon it.
                                            G. Macdonald

There is more of good nature than of good sense at the bottom of most marriages.
                                            Henry David Thoreau

MERIT

True merit, like a river, the deeper it is, the less noise it makes.
                                            Earl of Halifax

Real merit of any kind, cannot long be concealed; it will be discovered, and nothing can depreciate it but a man exhibiting it himself. It may not always be rewarded as it ought; but it will always be known.
                                            Earl of Chesterfield

If you wish your merit to be known, acknowledge that of other people.

Oriental Proverb

Charms strike the sight, but merit wins the soul.

Alexander Pope

METHOD

Method is like packing things in a box; a good packer will get in half as much again as a bad one.

Cecil

The first idea of method is a progressive transition from one step to another in any course.—If in the right course, it will be the true method; if in the wrong, we cannot hope to progress.

Samuel Taylor Coleridge

Be methodical if you would succeed in business, or in anything.—Have a work for every moment, and mind the moment's work.—Whatever your calling, master all its bearings and details, its principles, instruments, and applications.—Method is essential if you would get through your work easily and with economy of time.

W. Mathews

Method facilitates every kind of business, and by making it easy makes it agreeable, and also successful.

C. Simmons

MINORITIES

Government is everywhere to a great extent controlled by powerful minorities, with an interest distinct from that of the mass of the people.

Goldsworthy Lowes Dickinson

If by the mere force of numbers a majority should deprive a minority of any clearly written constitutional right, it might, in a moral point of view, justify revolution—certainly would if such a right were a vital one.

Abraham Lincoln

Minorities are individuals or groups of individuals especially qualified. The masses are the collection of people not specially qualified.

José Ortega y Gasset

The smallest number, with God and truth on their side, are weightier than thousands.

C. Simmons

MORTALITY

The mortality of mankind is but a part of the process of living—a step on the way to immortality.—Dying, to the good man, is but a brief sleep, from which he wakes to a perfection and fullness of life in eternity.

Tryon Edwards

When we see our enemies and friends gliding away before us, let us not forget that we are subject to the general law of mortality, and shall soon be where our doom will be fixed forever.

Johnson

Consider the lilies of the field, whose bloom is brief.—We are as they; like them we fade away, as doth the leaf.

Rossetti

All men think all mortal but themselves.

Young

MOTHER

The babe at first feeds upon the mother's bosom, but is always on her heart.

H. W. Beecher

God could not be everywhere, and therefore he made mothers.

Jewish saying

Stories first heard at a mother's knee are never wholly forgotten,—a little spring that never quite dries up in our journey through scorching years.

Ruffini

The dignity, the grandeur, the tenderness, the everlasting and divine significance of motherhood.

De Witt Talmage

MOTIVES

In the eye of that Supreme Being to whom our whole internal frame uncovered, motives and dispositions hold the place of actions.

Blair

If a man speaks or acts with pure thought, happiness follows him like a shadow that never leaves him.

Buddha

Many actions, like the Rhone, have two sources: one pure, the other impure.

Hare

The morality of an action depends upon the motive from which we act.

Johnson

NATIONS

In the youth of a state, arms do flourish; in the middle age, learning; and then both of them together for a time; in the declining age, mechanical arts and merchandise.

Francis Bacon

Individuals may form communities, but it is institutions alone that can create a nation.

Benjamin Disraeli

It is written in God's word, and in all the history of the race, that nations, if they live at all, live not by felicity of position, or soil, or climate, and not by abundance of material good, but by the living word of the living God.—The commandments of God are the bread of life for the nations.

R. D. Hitchcock

No nation can be destroyed while it possesses a good home life.

J. G. Holland

NATURE

Surely there is something in the unruffled calm of nature that overawes our little anxieties and doubts: the sight of the deep-blue sky, and the clustering stars above, seem to impart a quiet to the mind.

Jonathan Edwards

Nature is too thin a screen; the glory of the One breaks in everywhere.

Ralph Waldo Emerson

Nature is the living, visible garment of God.

Johann Wolfgang von Goethe

Nature is avariciously frugal; in matter, it allows no atom to elude its grasp; in mind, no thought or feeling to perish. It gathers up the fragments that nothing be lost.

David Thomas

OCCUPATION

The busy have no time for tears.

George Gordon, Lord Byron

Care is a sad disease; despondency a sadder, and discontent the saddest of the three: if we wish to be cured of all these together, next to seeking the divine support, the prescription is occupation.

The want of occupation is no less the plague of society, than of solitude.

Jean Jacques Rousseau

Indolence is a delightful but distressing state; we must be doing something to be happy. Action is no less necessary than thought to the instinctive tendencies of the human frame.

William Hazlitt

I take it to be a principal rule of life, not to be too much addicted to any one thing.

Terence

OLD AGE

All of us, as the years slip by, face increasingly the problem of living with the abiding subtractions of death. These create gaps which cannot be filled and leave us suddenly lonely in the midst of crowds.

John Mason Brown

As I approve of a youth that has something of the old man in him, so I am no less pleased with an old man that has something of the youth. He that follows this rule, may be old in body, but can never be so in mind.

Cicero

Old age is a tyrant who forbids, at the penalty of life, all the pleasures of youth.

Duc Francois de La Rochefoucauld

There is a peculiar beauty about godly old age—the beauty of holiness. Husband and wife who have fought the world side by side, who have made common stock of joy or sorrow, and become aged together, are not unfrequently found curiously alike in personal appearance, in pitch and tone of voice, just as twin pebbles on the beach, exposed to the same tidal influences, are each other's alter ego.

Alexander Smith

OPINION

The men of the past had convictions, while we moderns have only opinions.

Heinrich Heine

Social opinion is like a sharp knife. There are foolish people who regard it only with terror, and dare not touch or meddle with it; there are more foolish people, who, in rashness or defiance, seize it by the blade, and get cut and mangled for their pains; and there are wise people, who grasp it discreetly and boldly by the handle, and use it to carve out their own purposes.

Anna Jameson

There never was in the world two opinions alike, no more than two hairs or two grains. The most universal quality is diversity.

Montaigne

This history of human opinion is scarcely anything more than the history of human errors.

Voltaire

OPPORTUNITY

The Chinese write the word "crisis" with two characters. One means danger and the other means opportunity. Together they spell "crisis."

Saul D. Alinsky

The million little things that drop into our hands, the small opportunities each day brings, He leaves us free to use or abuse and goes unchanging along His silent way.

Helen Keller

God's best gift to us is not things, but opportunities.

Alice W. Rollins

Liberty requires opportunity to make a living—a living which gives man not only enough to live by, but something to live for.

Franklin D. Roosevelt

ORIGINALITY

Every human being is intended to have a character of his own; to be what no other is, and to do what no other can do.

William Ellery Channing

One couldn't carry on life comfortably without a little blindness to the fact that everything has been said better than we can put it ourselves.

George Eliot

It is better to create than to be learned; creating is the true essence of life.

Barthold G. Niebuhr

Originality is nothing but judicious imitation.—The most original writers borrowed one from another. The instruction we find in books is like fire. We fetch it from our neighbor's, kindle it at home, communicate it to others, and it becomes the property of all.

Voltaire

PARENTS

Honor thy parents, those that gave thee birth, and watched in tenderness thine earliest days, and trained thee up in youth, and loved in all. Honor, obey, and love in all. Honor, obey, and love them; it shall fill their souls with holy joy, and shall bring down God's richest blessing on thee; and in days to come, thy children, if they're given, shall honor thee, and fill thy life with peace.

Tryon Edwards

How many hopes and fears, how many ardent wishes and anxious apprehensions, are twisted together in the threads that connect the parent with the child!

S. G. Goodrich

Train up a child in the way he should go,/And when he is old he will not depart from it.

Proverbs 22:6

We speak of educating our children. Do we know that our children also educate us?

Lydia H. Sigourney

PARTING

Could we see when and where we are to meet again, we would be more tender when we bid our friends good-by.

Ouida

"Good-bye"—that is, "God be with you." Is this your earnest prayer in parting from your friends?

Never part without loving words to think of during your absence. It may be that you will not meet again in life.

Jean Paul [Johann Paul Friedrich Richter]

Farewell, God knows when we shall meet again.—I have a faint cold fear thrill through my veins, that almost freezes up the heat of life.

William Shakespeare

Adieu! I have too grieved a heart to take a tedious leave.

William Shakespeare

PAST

Study the past if you would divine the future.

Confucius

No poet, no artist of any art, has his complete meaning alone. His significance, his appreciation is the appreciation of his relation to the dead poets and artists.

T. S. Eliot

The future of a country is safe only in the hands of those to whom her past is dear.

William Ralph Inge

We ought not to look back unless it is to derive useful lessons from past errors, and for the purpose of profiting by dear bought experience.

George Washington

PATIENCE

Patience is power; with time and patience the mulberry leaf becomes silk.

Chinese Proverb

Life has such hard conditions that every dear and precious gift, every rare virtue, every genial endowment, love, hope, joy, wit, sprightliness, benevolence, must sometimes be put into the crucible to distil the one elixir—patience.

Gail Hamilton

The sincere and earnest approach of the Christian to the throne of the Almighty, teaches the best lesson of patience under affliction, since wherefore should we mock the Deity with supplications, when we insult him by murmuring under his decrees?

Walter Scott

How poor are they who have not patience! What wound did ever heal but by degrees.

William Shakespeare

PEACE

Peace is the golden wisp that binds the sheaf of blessings.

Katherine Lee Bates

Especially important it is to realize that there can be no assured peace and tranquility for any one nation except as it is achieved for all. So long as want, frustration, and a sense of injustice prevail among significant sections of earth, no other section can be wholly released from fear.

Dwight D. Eisenhower

"Peace I leave with you, My peace I give to you; not as the world gives do I give to you. Let not your heart be troubled, neither let it be afraid."

John 14:27

If every human being could be asked what he would rather have in life than anything else, a composite of all the answers would probably show that peace in the heart is what we really want.

Archibald Rutledge

PERFECTION

Perfection consists not in doing extraordinary things, but in doing ordinary things extraordinarily well. Neglect nothing; the most trivial action may be performed to God.

Angelique Arnauld

Bachelor's wives and old maid's children are always perfect.

Chamfort

Aim at perfection in everything, though in most things it is unattainable.—However, they who aim at it, and persevere, will come much nearer to it than those whose laziness and despondency make them give it up as unattainable.

Earl of Chesterfield

Perfection does not exist; to understand it is the triumph of human intelligence; to expect to possess it is the most dangerous kind of madness.

Alfred de Musset

PLEASURE

Worldly and sensual pleasures, for the most part, are short, false, and deceitful. Like drunkenness, they revenge the jolly madness of one hour with the sad repentance of many.

He who spends all his life in sport is like one who wears nothing but fringes, and eats nothing but sauces.

Richard Fuller

The greatest pleasure I know, is to do a good action by stealth, and have it found out by accident.

Charles Lamb

The pleasures of the world are deceitful; they promise more than they give. They trouble us in seeking them, they do not satisfy us when possessing them, and they make us despair in losing them.

Madame de Lambert

A life merely of pleasure, or chiefly of pleasure, is always a poor and worthless life, not worth the living; always unsatisfactory in its course, always miserable in its end.

Theodore Parker

PRAISE

Words of praise, indeed, are almost as necessary to warm a child into a congenial life as acts of kindness and affection. Judicious praise is to children what the sun is to flowers.

Bovee

Those who are greedy of praise prove that they are poor in merit.

Plutarch

Praise the LORD!
For it is good to sing praises to our God;
For it is pleasant, and praise is beautiful.

Psalm 147:1

Whenever you commend, add your reasons for doing so; it is this which distinguishes the approbation of a man of sense from the flattery of sycophants and admiration of fools.

Sir Richard Steele

PRAYER

Give us, we pray, the power to discern clearly right from wrong, and allow all our words and actions to be governed thereby, and by the laws of this land. Especially we pray that our concern shall be for all the people regardless of station, race or calling.

May cooperation be permitted and be the mutual aim of those

who, under the concepts of our Constitution, hold to differing political faiths; so that all may work for the good of our beloved country and Thy Glory. Amen.

Dwight D. Eisenhower

Certain thoughts are prayers. There are moments when, whatever be the attitude of the body, the soul is on its knees.

Victor Hugo

I have been driven many times to my knees by the overwhelming conviction that I had nowhere else to go. My own wisdom, and that of all about me, seemed insufficient for the day.

Abraham Lincoln

Prayer is not eloquence, but earnestness; not the definition of helplessness, but the feeling of it; not figures of speech, but earnestness of soul.

Hannah More

PRIDE

Pride thrust Nebuchadnezzar out of men's society, Saul out of his kingdom, Adam out of paradise, Haman out of court, and Lucifer out of heaven.

T. Adam

The devil did grin, for his darling sin is pride that apes humility.

Samuel Taylor Coleridge

We probably wouldn't worry about what people think of us if we could know how seldom they do.

Olin Miller

Let me give you the history of pride in three small chapters. The beginning of pride was in heaven. The continuance of pride is on earth. The end of pride is in hell. This history shows how unprofitable it is.

R. Newton

PRINCIPLES

Expedients are for the hour; principles for the ages.

H. W. Beecher

He who merely knows right principles is not equal to him who loves them.

Confucius

Principle is a passion for truth and right.

William Hazlitt

Our principles are the springs of our actions; our actions, the springs of our happiness or misery. Too much care, therefore, cannot be taken in forming our principles.

John Skelton

PROGRESS

All our progress is an unfolding, like the vegetable bud.—You have first an instinct, then an opinion, then a knowledge, as the plant has root, bud, and fruit.—Trust the instinct to the end, though you can render no reason.

Ralph Waldo Emerson

I am suffocated and lost when I have not the bright feeling of progression.

Margaret Fuller

There is no law of progress. Our future is in our own hands, to make or to mar. It will be an uphill fight to the end, and would we have it otherwise? Let no one suppose that evolution will ever exempt us from struggles. "You forget," said the Devil, with a chuckle, "that I have been evolving too."

William Ralph Inge

We are never present with, but always beyond ourselves.—Fear, desire, and hope are still pushing us on toward the future.

Montaigne

PURPOSE

The secret of success is constancy to purpose.

Benjamin Disraeli

Man proposes, but God disposes.

Thomas á Kempis

There is no road to success but through a clear strong purpose.—Nothing can take its place.—A purpose underlies character, culture, position, attainment of every sort.

T. T. Munger

It is the old lesson—a worthy purpose, patient energy for its accomplishment, a resoluteness undaunted by difficulties, and then success.

W. M. Punshon

RESPONSIBILITY

Responsibility walks hand in hand with capacity and power.

J. G. Holland

Responsibility educates.

Wendell Phillips

No matter how lofty you are in your department, the responsibility for what your lowliest assistant is doing is yours.

Bessie R. James and Mary
Waterstreet

The most important thought that I ever had was that of my individual responsibility to God.

Daniel Webster

RIGHTS

Freedom of speech does not travel exclusively on a one-way street marked "Search for Truth." It often enough travels on a one-way street marked "Private Profit," or on another marked "Anything to Win the Election."

Carl Lotus Becker

All men are endowed by their Creator with unalienable rights; among these are life, liberty, and the pursuit of happiness.

Thomas Jefferson

One of the grandest things in having rights is, that though they are your rights you may give them up.

George Macdonald

Never, with the Bible in our hands, can we deny rights to another, which, under the same circumstances, we would claim for ourselves.

G. Spring

SELF-IMPROVEMENT

If we do not better our civilization, our way of life, and our democracy, there will be no use trying to "save" them by fighting; they will crumble away under the very feet of our armies.

Anne Morrow Lindbergh

The improvement of our way of life is more important than the spreading of it. If we make it satisfactory enough, it will spread automatically. If we do not, no strength of arms can permanently impose it.

Charles A. Lindbergh

Begin to be now what you will be hereafter.

St. Jerome

By all means sometimes be alone; salute thyself; see what thy soul doth wear; dare to look in thy chest, and tumble up and down what thou findest there.

William Wordsworth

SELF-RESPECT

Self-respect,—that corner of all virtue.

Sir John Herschel

I care not so much what I am in the opinion of others as what I am in my own; I would be rich of myself and not by borrowing.

Montaigne

Above all things, reverence yourself.

Pythagoras

Who will adhere to him that abandons himself?

Sir Philip Sidney

SINCERITY

Sincerity is no test of truth—no evidence of correctness of conduct.—You may take poison sincerely believing it the needed medicine, but will it save your life?

Tryon Edwards

Sincerity is the indispensable ground of all conscientiousness, and by consequence of all heartfelt religion.

Immanuel Kant

To be sincere with ourselves is better and harder than to be painstakingly accurate with others.

Agnes Repplier

The shortest and surest way to live with honor in the world, is to be in reality what we would appear to be; all human virtues increase and strengthen themselves by the practice and experience of them.

Socrates

SUCCESS

Success is counted sweetest by those who ne'er succeed.

Emily Dickinson

Possessions, outward success, publicity, luxury—to me these have always been contemptible. I believe that a simple and unassuming manner of life is best for everyone, best both for the body and the mind.

Albert Einstein

Young man, the secret of my success is that at an early age I discovered I was not God.

Oliver Wendell Holmes

I have learned that success is to be measured not so much by the position that one has reached in life as by the obstacles which he has overcome while trying to succeed.

Booker T. Washington

SUFFERING

Night brings out stars, as sorrow shows us truths.

G. Bailey

To be born is to suffer: to grow old is to suffer: to die is to suffer: to lose what is loved is to suffer: to be tied to what is not loved is to suffer: to endure what is distasteful is to suffer. In short, all the results of individuality, of separate self-hood, necessarily involve pain or suffering.

Subhadra Bhikshu

We need to suffer that we may learn to pity.

L. E. Landon

Many are the afflictions of the righteous,/But the LORD delivers him out of them all.

Psalm 34:19

TALENT

Talent, like beauty, to be pardoned, must be obscure and unostentatious.

Lady Blessington

Great offices will have great talents, and God gives to every man the virtue, temper, understanding, taste, that lifts him into life, and lets him fall just in the niche he was ordained to fill.

William Cowper

The most valuable of all talents is that of never using two words when one will do.

Thomas Jefferson

Use what talents you possess: the woods would be very silent if no birds sang there except those that sang best.

Henry Van Dyke

TEACHING

Those who educate children well are more to be honored than even their parents, for these only give them life, those the art of living well.

Aristotle

Thoroughly to teach another is the best way to learn for yourself.

Tryon Edwards

Let our teaching be full of ideas. Hitherto it has been stuffed only with facts.

Anatole France

The teacher who is attempting to teach without inspiring the pupil with a desire to learn is hammering on cold iron.

Horace Mann

THANKFULNESS

Pride slays thanksgiving, but an humble mind is the soil out of which thanks naturally grow.—A proud man is seldom a grateful man, for he never thinks he gets as much as he deserves.

H. W. Beecher

The unthankful heart, like my finger in the sand, discovers no mercies; but let the thankful heart sweep through the day, and as the magnet finds the iron, so it will find, in every hour, some heavenly blessings, only the iron in God's sand is gold!

H. W. Beecher

The worship most acceptable to God comes from a thankful and cheerful heart.

Plutarch

God's goodness hath been great to thee.—Let never day nor night unhallowed pass but still remember what the Lord hath done.

William Shakespeare

TROUBLE

Most of the shadows of this life are caused by standing in your own sunshine.

Ralph Waldo Emerson

I have had many troubles in my life, but the worst of them never came.

James A. Garfield

The true way of softening one's troubles is to solace those of others.

Madame de Maintenon

Though I walk in the midst of trouble,
You will revive me;
You will stretch out Your hand
Against the wrath of my enemies,
And Your right hand will save me.

Psalm 138:7

TRUTH

What we have in us of the image of God is the love of truth and justice.

Demosthenes

Truth is the foundation of all knowledge and the cement of all societies.

John Dryden

Treat kindly every miserable truth that knocks begging at your door, otherwise you will some day fail to recognize Truth Himself when He comes in rags.

Austin O'Malley

It is easier to perceive error than to find truth, for the former lies on the surface and is easily seen, while the latter lies in the depth, where few are willing to search for it.

Johann Wolfgang von Goethe

UNDERSTANDING

The eye of the understanding is like the eye of the sense; for as you may see great objects through small crannies or holes, so you may see great axioms of nature through small and contemptible instances.

Francis Bacon

It is a common fault never to be satisfied with our fortune, nor dissatisfied with our understanding.

Duc Francois de La Rochefoucauld

The improvement of the understanding is for two ends; first, our own increase of knowledge; secondly, to enable us to deliver that knowledge to others.

John Locke

I hold myself indebted to any one from whose enlightened understanding another ray of knowledge communicates to mine.— Really to inform the mind is to correct and enlarge the heart.

Junius

USEFULNESS

Think that day lost, whose low descending sun views from thy hand no worthy action done.

Anonymous

We live in a world which is full of misery and ignorance, and the plain duty of each and all of us is to try to make the little corner he can influence somewhat less miserable and somewhat less ignorant than it was before he entered it.

Thomas H. Huxley

There is but one virtue—the eternal sacrifice of self.

George Sand

Try to make at least one person happy every day, and then in ten years you may have made three thousand, six hundred and fifty persons happy, or brightened a small town by your contribution to the fund of general enjoyment.

Sydney Smith

VIRTUE

If you can be well without health, you may be happy without virtue.

Edmund Burke

The virtue of a man ought to be measured not by his extraordinary exertions, but by his every-day conduct.

Blaise Pascal

Virtue is certainly the most noble and secure possession a man can have. Beauty is worn out by time or impaired by sickness—riches lead youth rather to destruction than welfare, and without prudence are soon lavished away; while virtue alone, the only good that is ever durable, always remains with the person that has once entertained her. She is preferable both to wealth and a noble extraction.

Richard Savage

We rarely like the virtues we have not.

William Shakespeare

WIFE

No man knows what the wife of his bosom is—what a ministering angel she is, until he has gone with her through the fiery trials of this world.

Washington Irving

Sole partner, and sole part of all my joys, dearer thyself than all.

John Milton

A faithful wife becomes the truest and tenderest friend, the balm of comfort, and the source of joy; through every various turn of life the same.

Savage

A good wife makes the cares of the world sit easy, and adds a sweetness to its pleasures: she is a man's best companion in prosperity, and his best if not only friend in adversity; the most careful preserver of his health, and the kindest attendant on his sickness; a faithful adviser in distress, a comforter in affliction, and a discreet manager of all his domestic affairs.

L. M. Stretch

WISDOM

The true test of intelligence is not how much we know how to do, but how we behave when we don't know what to do.

John Holt

The wise man is he who knows the relative value of things.

William Ralph Inge

Wisdom is to the mind what health is to the body.

Duc Francois de La Rochefoucauld

We learn wisdom from failure much more than from success. We often discover what will do by finding out what will not do, and probably he who never made a mistake never made a discovery.

Samuel Smiles

WISHES

Wishes are the parents of large families, but the children are generally inefficient and useless.—They are the source of idle and vain dreams, and of air castles which have no solid foundation.— The idle wish sends one on a vain journey from which he gains nothing but mental emptiness and discontent with his lot, and it may be, some rebukes of conscience, if it is sharp enough to see his folly.

Anonymous

Every wish is like a prayer with God.

Elizabeth Barrett Browning

I could write down twenty cases wherein I wished that God had done otherwise than he did, but which I now see, if I had had my own way, would have led to extensive mischief.

Cecil

What we ardently wish we soon believe.

Young

WORK

The man who works with his hands is a laborer.

The man who works with his hands and his brains is a craftsman.

The man who works with his hands, his brains and his heart is an artist.

Anonymous

A man is a worker. If he is not that he is nothing.

Joseph Conrad

As a cure for worrying, work is better than whiskey.

Thomas A. Edison

He who would really benefit mankind must reach them through their work.

Henry Ford

WORLD

It is a beautiful and a blessed world we live in, and while life lasts, to lose the enjoyment of it is a sin.

A. W. Chambers

To understand the world is wiser than to condemn it. To study the world is better than to shun it. To use the world is nobler than to abuse it. To make the world better, lovelier, and happier, is the noblest work of man or woman.

Duc Francois de La Rochefoucauld

The world is God's epistle to mankind—his thoughts are flashing upon us from every direction.

Plato

A good man and a wise man may at times be angry with the world, at times grieved for it; but be sure no man was ever discontented with the world who did his duty in it.

Robert Southey

WORSHIP

Give unto the LORD the glory due to His name;
Worship the LORD in the beauty of holiness.

Psalm 29:2

All the earth shall worship You
And sing praises to You;
They shall sing praises to Your name.

Psalm 66:4

Whatever makes us rejoice, makes us want to worship. We seem to want to tell God all about it, just as a child will take a new-found joy to its father and mother. Sorrow, too, should makes us want to worship. If we tell God, we are better for the telling.

Archibald Rutledge

One of the proofs of the divinity of our gospel is the preaching it has survived.

Woodrow Wilson

YOUTH

Universities are full of knowledge; the freshmen bring a little in and the seniors take none away, and knowledge accumulates.

Abbott L. Lowell

Nature makes boys and girls lovely to look upon so they can be tolerated until they acquire some sense.

William Lyon Phelps

Youth is a wonderful thing. What a crime to waste it on children.

George Bernard Shaw

For God's sake give me the young man who has brains enough to make a fool of himself.

Robert Louis Stevenson

NOTES

Chapter 9

[1]William F. Hobby, *How to Say It Better* (Nashville: Manuscript Press, 1983), 18.
[2]Stephen E. Lucas, *The Art of Public Speaking* (New York: Random House, 1983), 5.
[3]Pericles, quoted in Lucas, *Public Speaking.*

Chapter 10

[1]Quoted in Wilhelmina G. Hedde, William Norwood Brigance, and Victor M. Powell, *The New American Speech* (Philadelphia: J. B. Lippincott, 1983), 41.
[2]Virgil L. Baker and Ralph T. Eubanks, *Speech in Personal and Public Affairs* (New York: David McKay Company, Inc., 1968), 22.
[3]Kenneth McFarland, *Eloquence in Public Speaking* (Englewood Cliffs, New Jersey: Prentice-Hall, 1961), 57.
[4]Lucas, *Public Speaking,* 11, 13.

Chapter 12

[1]Eugene E. White, *Basic Public Speaking* (New York: Macmillan, 1984), 11.
[2]Lucas, *Public Speaking,* 54.
[3]Ibid., 67.

Chapter 13

[1]White, *Basic Speaking,* 78.
[2]Proodian, "There Are No Dull Subjects..." *Wall Street Journal,* January 14, 1985.
[3]William K. Grasty and Mary T. Newman, *Introduction to Basic Speech* (Beverly Hills, California: Glencoe Press, 1969), 56.
[4]Lucas, *Public Speaking,* 118.
[5]White, *Basic Speaking,* 47.
[6]Ibid., 48.
[7]Wayne C. Minnick, *Public Speaking* (Boston: Houghton Mifflin, 1983), 132.
[8]Hedde, Brigance, and Powell, *American Speech,* 128.

[9]Lucas, *Public Speaking*, 274.
[10]Grasty and Newman, *Basic Speech*, 55.
[11]Quoted by Ralph S. Pomeroy in *Speaking from Experience* (New York: Harper & Row, 1977), 97-98.
[12]Lucas, *Public Speaking*, 124.
[13]Minnick, *Speaking*, 51, 119.
[14]Lucas, *Public Speaking*, 254.
[15]Ibid., 254.

Chapter 14

[1]Baker and Eubanks, *Speech in Public Affairs*, 37.
[2]Bess Sondel, *Everyday Speech: How to Say What You Mean* (New York: Harper & Row, 1950), 115.
[3]White, *Basic Speaking*, 79.
[4]Ibid.
[5]Baker and Eubanks, *Speech in Public Affairs*, 149.
[6]Minnick, *Speaking*, 58.
[7]White, *Basic Speaking*, 82.
[8]Lucas, *Public Speaking*, 87.
[9]White, *Basic Speaking*, 83.
[10]Hobby, *Say It Better*, 35.
[11]Lucas, *Public Speaking*, 90.
[12]Ibid., 89.
[13]White, *Basic Speaking*, 84.
[14]Sondel, *Everyday Speech*, 97.
[15]White, *Basic Speaking*, 86.

Chapter 15

[1]Lucas, *Public Speaking*, 53.
[2]Hobby, *Say It Better*, 142.
[3]Sondel, *Everyday Speech*, 14.
[4]White, *Basic Speaking*, 122.
[5]Ibid., 147.
[6]Ibid., 171.
[7]Proodian, "No Dull Subjects."
[8]Keith Spicer, *Winging It* (Garden City, New York: Doubleday, 1982), 21.
[9]Hobby, *Say It Better*, 45.
[10]McFarland, *Eloquence*, 109.
[11]Hobby, *Say It Better*, 109.
[12]Sondel, *Everyday Speech*, 163.
[13]Hobby, *Say It Better*, 106.
[14]Spicer, *Winging It*, 131.
[15]Ibid., 130.
[16]White, *Basic Speaking*, 12.
[17]Ibid.
[18]Sondel, *Everyday Speech*, 104.
[19]Ibid., 123.
[20]Proodian, "No Dull Subjects."

[21]Hobby, *Say It Better,* 118.
[22]White, *Basic Speaking,* 13.
[23]Spicer, *Winging It,* 233.
[24]Hobby, *Say It Better,* 83.

Chapter 16

[1]Sondel, *Everday Speech,* 87.
[2]Hobby, *Say It Better,* 67.
[3]Ibid., 84.
[4]Ibid., 127.
[5]Ibid., 126.
[6]Ibid.
[7]Ibid., 53.
[8]Ibid., 124.

Chapter 17

[1]Spicer, *Winging It,* 6.
[2]McFarland, *Eloquence,* 6.
[3]Batsell Barrett Baxter, *Speaking for the Master* (New York: MacMillan, 1972), 12.
[4]Spicer, *Winging It,* 14.
[5]White, *Basic Speaking,* 7.
[6]Hobby, *Say It Better,* 68.
[7]Sondel, *Everday Speech,* 131.
[8]Ibid.
[9]Hobby, *Say It Better,* 29.
[10]Baxter, *Say It Better,* 12.
[11]Ibid.
[12]Hobby, *Say It Better,* 43.
[13]Baxter, *The Master,* 63.
[14]Hobby, *Say It Better,* 41.
[15]Ibid.
[16]Proodian, "No Dull Subjects," 14.
[17]Hobby, *Say It Better,* 123.
[18]Sondel, *Everday Speech,* 25.
[19]Ibid., 167.
[20]White, *Basic Speaking,* 134.
[21]Lucas, *Public Speaking,* 13.
[22]Hobby, *Say It Better,* 120.
[23]Ibid., 51.
[24]Ibid., 48.
[25]Lucas, *Public Speaking,* 11.
[26]McFarland, *Eloquence,* 13.
[27]Lucas, *Public Speaking,* 14.

Chapter 18

[1]Information taken from material offered by the United States Navy Recruiting Service, RAD 67915, U.S. Government Printing Office: 1967, 260-412.

Chapter 19

[1]Steven E. Lucas, *The Art of Public Speaking* (New York: Random House, 1983), 327.

Chapter 20

[1]Reprinted with permission of Gregory Peck and the Academy of Motion Picture Arts and Sciences. Copyright 1982 by the Academy of Motion Picture Arts and Sciences.

Chapter 21

[1]Reprinted with permission of Joan Daves, © 1964 by the Nobel Foundation.

Chapter 32

[1]Elizabeth L. Post, *Emily Post's Etiquette*, 12th revised edition (New York: Funk and Wagnalls, 1969), 34-36.

Chapter 34

[1]William Hobby, *How to Say It Better* (Nashville: Manuscript Press, 1983), 136-38.
[2]Quoted by Batsell Barrett Baxter, *Speaking for the Master* (New York: Macmillan, 1972), 37-41.